BAsics

from the talks and writings of
Bob Avakian

RCP Publications

FIRST EDITION
First printing: 2011
Second printing: 2013

ISBN: 978-0-89851-010-2

RCP Publications
P.O. Box 3486
Merchandise Mart
Chicago, Illinois 60654-0486
revcom.us

CONTENTS

CHAPTER 1
A WORLDWIDE SYSTEM OF EXPLOITATION AND OPPRESSION

#1

There would be no United States as we now know it today without slavery. That is a simple and basic truth.

Communism and Jeffersonian Democracy, 2008

#2

Now, of course, slavery was not the only factor that played a significant part in the emergence of the U.S. as a world power, whose economic strength underlies its massive military force. A major historical factor in all this was the theft of land, on a massive scale, from Mexico as well as from native peoples. But, in turn, much of that conquest of land was, for a long period of time up until the Civil War, largely to expand the slave system. "Remember the Alamo," we are always reminded. Well, many of the "heroes" of the Alamo were slave traders and slave chasers....And expanding the slave system was a major aim of the overall war with Mexico, although that war also led to the westward expansion of the developing capitalist system centered in the northern United States.

Communism and Jeffersonian Democracy

#3

The essence of what exists in the U.S. is not democracy but capitalism-imperialism and political structures to enforce that capitalism-imperialism. What the U.S. spreads around the world is not democracy, but imperialism and political structures to enforce that imperialism.

Revolution #43, April 16, 2006

#4

Not only did slavery play a major role in the historical development of the U.S., but the wealth and power of the U.S. rests today on a worldwide system of imperialist exploitation that ensnares hundreds of millions, and ultimately billions, of people in conditions hardly better than those of slaves. Now, if this seems like an extreme or extravagant claim, think about the tens of millions of children throughout the Third World who, from a very, very early age, are working nearly every day of the year—as the slaves on the southern plantations in the United States used to say, "from can't see in the morning, till can't see at night"—until they've been physically used up....These are conditions very similar to outright slavery....This includes overt sexual harassment of women, and many other degradations as well.

All this is the foundation on which the imperialist system rests, with U.S. imperialism now sitting atop it all.

Communism and Jeffersonian Democracy

#5

It is not uncommon to hear these days, from government officials and others, that only 1 percent of the population is in the U.S. military but that this 1 percent is fighting for the freedom of the other 99 percent. The truth, however, is this: That 1 percent, in the military, is in reality fighting for the other 1 percent: the big capitalist-imperialists who run this country—who control the economy, the political system, the military, the media, and the other key institutions—and who dominate large parts of the world, wreaking havoc and causing great suffering for literally billions of people. It is the "freedom" of these capitalist-imperialists—their freedom to exploit, oppress, and plunder—that this 1 percent in the military is actually killing and sometimes dying for.

Revolution #220, December 19, 2010

#6

Imperialism means huge monopolies and financial institutions controlling the economies and the political systems—and the lives of people—not just in one country but all over the world. Imperialism means parasitic exploiters who oppress hundreds of millions of people and condemn them to untold misery; parasitic financiers who can cause millions to starve just by pressing a computer key and thereby shifting vast amounts of wealth from one place to another. Imperialism means war—war to put down the resistance and rebellion of the oppressed, and war between rival imperialist states—it means the leaders of these states can condemn humanity to unbelievable devastation, perhaps even total annihilation, with the push of a button.

Imperialism is capitalism at the stage where its basic contradictions have been raised to tremendously explosive levels. But imperialism also means that there will be revolution—the oppressed rising up to overthrow their exploiters and tormentors—and that this revolution will be a worldwide struggle to sweep away the global monster, imperialism.

> "We Have a World to Win," *Revolutionary Worker* #1032,
> November 28, 1999 (quote originally published 1985)

#7

These imperialists make the Godfather look like Mary Poppins.

> *Bullets, From the Writings, Speeches, & Interviews of Bob Avakian,*
> *Chairman of the Revolutionary Communist Party, USA,* 1985

#8

There is a semi-official narrative about the history and the "greatness" of America, which says that this greatness of America lies in the freedom and ingenuity of its people, and above all in a system that gives encouragement and reward to these qualities. Now, in opposition to this semi-official narrative about the greatness of America, the reality is that—to return to one fundamental aspect of all this—slavery has been an indispensable part of the foundation for the "freedom and prosperity" of the USA. The combination of freedom and prosperity is, as we know, still today, and in some ways today more than ever, proclaimed as the unique quality and the special destiny and mission of the United States and its role in the world. And this stands in stark contradiction to the fact that without slavery, none of this—not even the bourgeois-democratic freedoms, let alone the prosperity—would have been possible, not only in the southern United States but in the North as well, in the country as a whole and in its development and emergence as a world economic and military power.

Communism and Jeffersonian Democracy

#9

They pontificate about "Responsibility"...how the lack of it is corrupting the youth and the people generally in the U.S. They insist that people must take responsibility for the choices they make in life. But why is it that, for the class of people Bennett* represents, the choices

---

* William Bennett is a major right-wing ideologue who has held high-level positions in Republican administrations.

involve things like whether to close down factories
in this or that area and whether to invest billions in
Mexico or South Korea, or what kinds of austerity
measures to impose on Peru, or how to wage war
against Iraq, or when to invade Panama or Haiti? While
for people in a country like the U.S. who are part of
what is broadly referred to as "the middle class," the
choices may be between accepting a cut in pay or losing
their job, or deciding whether to go deeper into debt to
help their kids get through college. And for millions in
the ghettos and barrios of the U.S., the choices involve
things like trying to get a minimum-wage job vs. going
on welfare, or turning to crime—or having to fight
in one of those wars the ruling class decides to wage.
And meanwhile, a young girl in Thailand—maybe as
young as 9 or 10—has the "choice" between slaving in
suffocating squalor in factories making clothes or toys
for export to countries like the U.S., or being forced into
a brothel to be sold for sex to traveling businessmen
from Japan, Europe, and the U.S.! It is the worldwide
system of capitalist imperialism and its economic,
social, and political relations of oppression that have
shaped these different choices for different classes and
groupings of people.

Preaching from a Pulpit of Bones, We Need Morality
But Not Traditional *Morality, 1999*

#10

Look at all these beautiful children who are female in
the world. And in addition to all the other outrages
which I have referred to, in terms of children
throughout the slums and shantytowns of the Third
World, in addition to all the horrors that will be
heaped on them—the actual living in garbage and
human waste in the hundreds of millions as their
fate, laid out before them, yes, even before they are
born—there is, on top of this, for those children who
are born female, the horror of everything that this
will bring simply because they are female in a world
of male domination. And this is true not only in the
Third World. In "modern" countries like the U.S. as
well, the statistics barely capture it: the millions who
will be raped; the millions more who will be routinely
demeaned, deceived, degraded, and all too often
brutalized by those who are supposed to be their most
intimate lovers; the way in which so many women
will be shamed, hounded and harassed if they seek
to exercise reproductive rights through abortion, or
even birth control; the many who will be forced into
prostitution and pornography; and all those who—if
they do not have that particular fate, and even if they
achieve some success in this "new world" where
supposedly there are no barriers for women—will
be surrounded on every side, and insulted at every
moment, by a society and a culture which degrades

women, on the streets, in the schools and workplaces, in the home, on a daily basis and in countless ways.

Unresolved Contradictions, Driving Forces for Revolution – Part III: "The New Synthesis and the Woman Question: The Emancipation of Women and the Communist Revolution – Further Leaps and Radical Ruptures," *Revolution* #194, March 7, 2010

#11

Determination decides who makes it out of the ghetto— now there is a tired old cliché, at its worst, on every level. This is like looking at millions of people being put through a meatgrinder and instead of focusing on the fact that the great majority are chewed to pieces, concentrating instead on the few who slip through in one piece and then on top of it all, using this to say that "the meatgrinder works"!

"The 'City Game' – And the City, No Game," *Revolution* #144, October 5, 2008 (quote originally published 1983)

#12

If you want to talk about who owes whom—if you keep in mind everything the capitalists (as well as the slaveowners) have accumulated through all the labor Black people have carried out in this country and the privileges that have been passed out to people on that basis—there wouldn't even *be* a U.S. imperialism as there is today if it weren't for the exploitation of Black people under this system. Not that the exploitation of Black people is the whole of it—there has been a lot of other people exploited, both in the U.S. and internationally, by this ruling class. But there wouldn't be a U.S. imperialism in the way there is today if it weren't for the exploitation of Black people under slavery and then after slavery in the sharecropping system and in the plants and other workplaces in a kind of caste-like oppression in the cities.

"Slavery: Yesterday and Today," *Revolution* #78, February 11, 2007 (quote originally published 1997)

#13

No more generations of our youth, here and all around the world, whose life is over, whose fate has been sealed, who have been condemned to an early death or a life of misery and brutality, whom the system has destined for oppression and oblivion even before they are born. I say no more of that.

Revolution: Why It's Necessary, Why It's Possible, What It's All About, a film of a talk by Bob Avakian. Available at revolutiontalk.net and in a DVD set from RCP Publications.

#14

Now I can just hear these reactionary fools saying, "Well, Bob, answer me this. If this country is so terrible, why do people come here from all over the world? Why are so many people trying to get in, not get out?"...Why? I'll tell you why. Because you have fucked up the rest of the world even worse than what you have done in this country. You have made it impossible for many people to live in their own countries as part of gaining your riches and power.

Revolution – a film of a talk by Bob Avakian

#15

But then, you know, capitalism still has its needs internationally and within the U.S., so it brings in these waves of immigrants and exploits them and rewrites or blots out history and turns people against each other. It doesn't tell these immigrants, who see a lot of Black people who've been pushed out of these jobs and are hanging on the corner, "By the way, those people went through this whole process a couple of generations ago; now we've got them in a different position and we're bringing you in so we can exploit you because the dynamics have gone that kind of way and we've developed policy in relation to that." No, they don't tell them that.

Question and Answer Session of the 7 *Talks by Bob Avakian*, 2006, excerpt transcribed in *Revolution* #78, February 11, 2007

#16

Now, sometimes you see these fools get up, you know, like these ranchers and all this kind of shit, and you can imagine "W" down there on his ranch. And they say things like "I'm a self-made man. Nobody gave me anything. I did it all myself." Yeah, you're a "self-made man." All the clothes you're wearing, everything you're using is made by other people. The machinery you're driving around, the rifle you own was made by other people. Everything you have and use is made by other people. And right now, you're exploiting

Mexican immigrants on your ranch. And you're sitting on land that was stolen from native peoples in the first place. But you're a "self-made man."

Revolution – a film of a talk by Bob Avakian

#17

Recently I was reading an essay called "Disarming Images" about an exhibit of art for nuclear disarmament which was held in the early 1980s. And I noticed that the author of this essay points out that according to the dictionary, *Webster's Third International Dictionary*, the name "bikini" given to the bathing suit comes from comparing "the effects of a scantily clad woman to the effects of an atomic bomb." When you think about this, and you think about the horrendous death, destruction, mutilation and suffering alive before dying that was caused by the atomic bombs that the U.S. dropped on Japan, and what would result from the much more powerful nuclear weapons these monsters have today—when you think about all that, and you think about the reasons for naming the bikini after all that, and what kind of view of women this promotes—do you need any other proof about how sick this system is, and how sick is the dominant culture it produces and promotes?

Revolution – a film of a talk by Bob Avakian

#18

The Black people, the youth, with their pants hanging down around their knees, their hats on backwards, their swagger, much of which I admire, weren't the ones who picked the jobs up and took them out of the ghetto. The people filling the prisons, the people in the gangs weren't the ones who took the jobs and moved them away. They were not the ones who, when Black people went chasing jobs, relocated them over the decades, discriminated against them, brought the police out to harass them and made it very difficult for them to get a job and keep a job under those circumstances.

None of that was done by the masses whom Bill Cosby so cheaply chooses to attack in this way. These were conditions that were caused by the dynamics of capitalist accumulation in its international dimension as well as within the country and by conscious policies of ruling class politicians in line with this.

> "Conservatism, Christian Fundamentalism, Liberalism and Paternalism...Bill Cosby and Bill Clinton...Not All 'Right' But All Wrong!" from the *7 Talks by Bob Avakian*

#19

The bourgeoisie (capitalist class) presides over a system in which people are compelled by necessity— by the fundamental workings and dynamics of that system of capitalism—to compete with each other in a thousand ways, and this system too in a thousand

ways promotes and rewards selfishness and surviving,
and if possible thriving, at the expense of others.
"Survivor"!—think what that television show is about
and promotes. In the U.S., in particular, all this takes
the form of extreme individualism and, along with that,
a grotesque celebration of "winners" and denigration
of "losers"—nobody has any use for a loser, and to the
winner go the spoils. At every turn, these values and
this worldview—serving this system of capitalism—are
promoted through the pervasive reach and influence of
the media, and culture in general, which are controlled
and dominated by this same ruling bourgeoisie. And
if all that is not enough, the functioning of this system
is backed up, after all, by the armed power of the
state, embodying the rule of this same capitalist class,
enforcing and reinforcing the workings of this system
and how this impels, and in many ways compels,
people to think only, or overwhelmingly and before
everything else, of self and the constant striving to gain
advantage over others.

And then, with all this in effect, the bourgeoisie and
the political theorists and philosophers (such as they
are), as well as the various commentators, pundits,
and other "opinion makers" who express the outlook
of the bourgeoisie, relentlessly broadcast the "brilliant
revelation" that, in this society, most people are selfish!
And that is not all: They incessantly proclaim that this

is some universal and unchangeable human character, or "human nature"—which makes it so that, lo and behold, the only possible system is the very one which generates and perpetuates this "human nature"!

Birds Cannot Give Birth to Crocodiles,
But Humanity Can Soar Beyond the Horizon – Part 1:
"Revolution and the State," *Revolution*, 2011

#20

One example that I've cited before...is the question of the "right to eat." Or why, in reality, under this system, there is <u>not</u> a "right to eat." Now, people can proclaim the "right to eat," but there is no such right with the workings of this system. You cannot actually implement that as a right, given the dynamics of capitalism and the way in which, as we've seen illustrated very dramatically of late, it creates unemployment. It creates and maintains massive impoverishment. (To a certain extent, even while there is significant poverty in the imperialist countries, that is to some degree offset and masked by the extent of parasitism there; imperialism "feeds off" the extreme exploitation of people in the Third World in particular, and some of the "spoils" from this "filter down" in significant ways to the middle strata especially. But, if you look at the world as a whole, capitalism creates and maintains tremendous impoverishment.)

Many, many people cannot find enough to eat and cannot eat in a way that enables them to be healthy—and in general they cannot maintain conditions that enable them to be healthy. So even right down to something as basic as "the right to eat"—people don't have that right under capitalism. If you were to declare it as a right, and people were to act on this and simply started going to where the food is sold as commodities and declaring "we have a more fundamental right than your right to distribute things as commodities and to accumulate capital—we have a right to eat"—and if they started taking the food, well then we know what would happen, and what has happened whenever people do this: "looters, shoot them down in the street."

Birds Cannot Give Birth to Crocodiles, But Humanity Can Soar Beyond the Horizon – Part 1, *Revolution* #218, November 28, 2010

#21

You can think of this in terms of politics and the state: If you didn't have, not only laws but a state apparatus of repression with the armed forces, the police, the courts, the prisons, the bureaucracies, the administrative function—if you didn't have that, how would you maintain the basic economic relations of exploitation and the basic social relations that go along with that? How would you maintain the domination of men over women, the domination of certain nationalities or "races" over others, if you did not have a superstructure to enforce that, or if that superstructure—the politics, the ideology and culture that is promoted, the morality promoted among people—were out of alignment with those social and, fundamentally, those economic relations? Once again, you wouldn't be able to maintain the order, stability and functioning of the system.

This is fundamentally why a system of this kind cannot be reformed. This goes back to the point that's in the Revolution talk about systems, and how they have certain dynamics and "rules." You can't just play any card you want in a card game or slap a domino down any time you want, anywhere you want, because the whole thing will come unraveled. And you can't have, as any significant phenomenon, cooperative economic relations in a system that operates on the dynamics of commodity production and exchange in which labor power itself, the ability to work, is a commodity.

A lot of reformist social democrats will talk in these terms: "Let's have real democracy in the superstructure" (they don't generally use terms like "superstructure," but that's the essence of what they mean) "and then," they'll say, "on that basis let's 'democratize' the economy." What would happen if you tried to implement this "democratization" of the economic base? That economic base would still be operating on the basis of, would still be driven by, the anarchy of commodity production and exchange in

which, once again, labor power is also a commodity—
in fact, the most basic commodity in capitalist
relations and capitalist society—and soon your
"democratization" of the economy would completely
break down, because the dynamics of commodity
production and exchange would mean that some would
fare better than others, some would beat out others—
plus you have the whole international arena where all
this would be going on.

*Birds Cannot Give Birth to Crocodiles, But Humanity Can Soar
Beyond the Horizon* – Part 1, *Revolution* #218, November 28, 2010

#22

In a world marked by profound class divisions and
social inequality, to talk about "democracy"—without
talking about the *class nature* of that democracy and
which class it serves—is meaningless, and worse.
So long as society is divided into classes, there can
be no "democracy for all": one class or another will
rule, and it will uphold and promote that kind of
democracy which serves its interests and goals. The
question is: *which class* will rule and whether its rule,
and its system of democracy, will serve the *continuation*,
or the eventual *abolition*, of class divisions and the
corresponding relations of exploitation, oppression and
inequality.

As quoted in the *Constitution of the
Revolutionary Communist Party, USA*, 2008
(quote originally published 2004)

#23

When a monopoly of political power—and, in a
concentrated way, the monopoly of "legitimate" armed
force—is in the hands of one group in society, and that
group excludes others from that monopoly of power
and force, then that is a **dictatorship** of the ruling
group—or class—regardless of whether or not that
ruling group allows those it excludes from power, and
over whom it rules in fact, to take part in elections to
vote for different representatives of the ruling class, as
happens in the U.S. and a number of other countries.
Political rule in the U.S., regardless of whether or
not there is an open and undisguised tyranny, is and
always has been a *bourgeois dictatorship, a dictatorship
of the ruling capitalist class* (or, in the early history of
the U.S., before the defeat and abolition of the slave
system, through the Civil War, what existed was the
dictatorship of the ruling *classes*—the slaveowning as
well as the capitalist class, or bourgeoisie).

> *Making Revolution and Emancipating Humanity* – Part 1:
> "Beyond the Narrow Horizon of Bourgeois Right,"
> *Revolution* #106, October 28, 2007

#24

The role of the police is not to serve and protect the
people. It is to serve and protect the system that rules
over the people. To enforce the relations of exploitation
and oppression, the conditions of poverty, misery and
degradation into which the system has cast people and

is determined to keep people in. The law and order the police are about, with all of their brutality and murder, is the law and the order that enforces all this oppression and madness.

Revolution – a film of a talk by Bob Avakian

#25

What a world! What a system and what a ruling class where "young earth creationists" and other reactionary cretins are allowed to have a major impact in influencing what is taught in the public schools— and apparently no higher political (ruling class) authority is willing or able to step in and declare, and act decisively to effect, that this cannot and will not be allowed, that it is simply impermissible for dangerous lunacy like this to be promoted as public policy and for people who promote such lunacy to sit on influential decision-making bodies.

All this provides yet another profound illustration of the fact that this ruling class has objectively forfeited any right to rule and to determine the direction of society—and to significantly influence the course of the world and the fate of humanity overall.

"Some Observations on the Culture Wars: Textbooks, Movies, Sham Shakespearean Tragedies and Crude Lies," *Revolution* #198, April 11, 2010

#26

As I have said a number of times: These reactionaries should not even be allowed to use "conservative" to describe themselves. We should say, "Conservative, my ass, these people are Nazis."

The Coming Civil War and Repolarization for Revolution
in the Present Era, Revolution #2, May 15, 2005

#27

And in this greatest of all possible countries, despite a recent Supreme Court decision which finally overturned a sodomy law, in Texas, that made it a crime for two people of the same sex to have sexual relations with each other—despite this Supreme Court decision, it remains a fact that those whose sexual orientation does not conform to the dominant male-female relations, or who in one way or another do not fit the stereotypes of what a man and a woman is supposed to be in this society—they are cruelly persecuted and discriminated against and often subjected to vicious and brutal attacks.

Revolution – a film of a talk by Bob Avakian

#28

What we see in contention here with Jihad on the one hand and McWorld/McCrusade on the other hand, are historically outmoded strata among colonized and oppressed humanity up against historically outmoded ruling strata of the imperialist system. These two reactionary poles <u>reinforce</u> each other, even while opposing each other. If you side with either of these "outmodeds," you end up strengthening both.

While this is a very important formulation and is crucial to understanding much of the dynamics driving things in the world in this period, at the same time we do have to be clear about which of these "historically outmodeds" has done the greater damage and poses the greater threat to humanity: It is the historically outmoded ruling strata of the imperialist system, and in particular the U.S. imperialists.

Bringing Forward Another Way, Revolution #86, April 29, 2007

#29

This system and those who rule over it are not capable of carrying out economic development to meet the needs of the people now, while balancing that with the needs of future generations and requirements of safeguarding the environment. They care nothing for the rich diversity of the earth and its species, for the treasures this contains, except when and where they can turn this into profit for themselves....These people are not fit to be the caretakers of the earth.

Revolution – a film of a talk by Bob Avakian

#30

And, as we know, they've always got excuses. People who rule in this way have to have a lot of excuses.

The ruling class and its apologists in this country will say: "We had to do certain things—pulling off a coup and putting the butcher Pinochet in power in Chile, doing the same kind of thing in Guatemala and Indonesia, Iran and other places—because of a greater evil, you see." "We were up against a greater evil," is a constant refrain of theirs. Today it's Islamic fundamentalism or "Islamo fascism." Previously it was other forms of "totalitarianism"—and, of course, communism in particular.

Well, leaving aside for the moment the distortions and slanders of what communism, the communist movement, and the experience of socialist states have actually been about, let's speak to this argument. Okay, then, what about the Philippines? You invaded the Philippines at the end of the 19th century, betrayed your promises to the people in the Philippines fighting for independence, waged a war of aggression to colonize the Philippines, massacred Philippine people in the hundreds of thousands and carried out unspeakable atrocities in the process—not just murdering people but parading around with the body parts of those who were killed, and all the rest that is so characteristic of your armed forces. Where was the Soviet Union then? Where was the People's Republic of China, when you did all this? They didn't even exist yet.

Or let's go back a little further. What about the genocide against the native peoples (the original peoples on this continent)? What about the enslavement of the African peoples, in the millions and millions, and all the consequences of that? Guess what? Karl Marx wasn't even born when you started doing that.

Your answer that you have done these things in response to greater evils is merely covering up a fundamental truth: I don't like to use the word evil (especially because of its religious connotations or "echoes"), but if "evil" has any meaning *you are it*. You and your system are the concentration in the modern world of the horrors of what humanity is put through, and the *fundamental cause* of the horrors that humanity is put through. And you have been carrying this out for centuries now—this has been carried out from the beginning of this country (and in the period of European settlement and conquest that led to the establishment of this country).

Making Revolution and Emancipating Humanity – Part 1,
Revolution #112, December 16, 2007

#31

If you can conceive of a world without America— without everything America stands for and everything it does in the world—then you've already taken great strides and begun to get at least a glimpse of a whole new world. If you can envision a world

without any imperialism, exploitation, oppression—
and the whole philosophy that rationalizes it—a
world without division into classes or even different
nations, and all the narrow-minded, selfish,
outmoded ideas that uphold this; if you can envision
all this, then you have the basis for proletarian
internationalism. And once you have raised your
sights to all this, how could you not feel compelled
to take an active part in the world historic struggle to
realize it; why would you want to lower your sights
to anything less?

Revolution #169, June 28, 2009
(quote originally published 1985)

Supplement

Reform or Revolution
Questions of Orientation,
Questions of Morality

Revolution #32, January 29, 2006, posted at revcom.us

Editor's note: The following is an excerpt from a talk given by Bob Avakian to a group of Party members and supporters in 2005.

Now, when you come up against the great gulf that often, and even generally, exists between the conditions and the suffering of the masses of people, on the one hand, and what you are able to do about that at any given point—when you run up against that repeatedly, everyone feels a definite pull which expresses itself in moral terms: how can you stand by and not do something about what's happening to the masses of people? As I have said a number of times, I have enormous respect for people who do things like volunteer for Doctors Without Borders. But the fact is that while they're doing what they're doing, and even with the good they do, this is being engulfed and overwhelmed by a tsunami of suffering (metaphorically speaking and sometimes literally) that's brought forth by larger objective forces.

When I was younger, I considered being a doctor or a lawyer, not to make money and get on the golf course, but because I knew there were many people who needed good medical care and people who were victimized by the so-called legal system who could use an advocate who really would be an advocate and a fighter for them. But at a certain point I came to understand that, while I would be helping a few people, and even if I threw myself into it, much greater numbers of people would find themselves in the position of needing these services—far beyond what I, and others, could do to help them—and it would just be perpetuated forever, and the conditions would get worse. And once you understand this, you can't look yourself in the mirror and do anything less than what you understand, if you're going to be consistent and follow through on your own principles.

So, yes, there's a moral dimension here. How can you sit by and watch people die of diseases that are preventable, not just in the Third World, but right down the street from you? How can you "sit by"? How can you not immediately try to do something about that? But moralities are a reflection of class outlooks, ultimately. They are a reflection of your understanding of reality, which takes a class expression in class society, in an ultimate and fundamental sense. And there is a morality that corresponds not to reformism and seeking merely to mitigate the conditions and the suffering of masses of people—not merely to addressing some, and only some, of the symptoms of that suffering—but to uprooting and abolishing the *causes* of that suffering. This morality corresponds to a revolutionary understanding, that we cannot eliminate the suffering of the masses, and in fact it's only going to get worse, as long as this capitalist-imperialist system remains.

This doesn't mean that it is unimportant to address particular abuses, or that mass resistance to particular forms of oppression is not important. Far from it. The basic point that Marx emphasized is profoundly true: If the masses don't fight back and resist their oppression, even short of revolution, they will be crushed and reduced to a broken mass and will be incapable of rising up for any higher thing. But, as a fundamental point of orientation, we have to grasp firmly the truth that, despite the best and most heroic and self-sacrificing efforts, it is not possible, within the framework of this system, even to really alleviate, let alone eliminate, the suffering and the causes of the suffering of the masses of people. And our morality has to flow from that.

Let me give you an analogy. Let's say you went back several centuries, somewhat like *Connecticut Yankee in King Arthur's Court*. Let's say in this case you went back to the time of the plagues in Europe that wiped out huge swaths of the population. And the most people knew to do then was to try to quarantine and stay away from people infected with the plague. Then, looking at all these people dying of the plague, if you were a good-hearted person perhaps you would take wet towels and put them on the foreheads of the people who were dying, or take some other steps to try to minimize their suffering to some degree. And maybe you would do what you could to keep the disease from spreading.

But let's say that, as a person from the present time, you know that the plague could actually be cured, fairly easily, with antibiotics, if they were administered in time. And, further extending and elaborating the analogy, let's imagine that somehow there were antibiotics back in that time—of course, in reality antibiotics did not exist and the scientific understanding had not been developed to produce antibiotics until more recent times, but let's say that somehow these antibiotics also existed back then: let's put into our scenario some other people who had also gone back in time from the present age and had taken with them a big stash of antibiotics, which could prevent the millions of deaths that were caused by the plague several centuries ago. But these other time-travelers were monopolizing the ownership of these antibiotics and had organized and paid an armed force of thugs to guard this stash of antibiotics, and were refusing to distribute any of these antibiotics unless they could profit from it, by charging a price that most of the people could not afford.

Now, knowing this, which way would people be better served: by continuing to put towels on the foreheads of the fevered people, or by organizing people to storm the compound where the antibiotics were being hoarded, seize the antibiotics and distribute them among the people?

This is, by analogy, the essential difference between reform and revolution. And our morality flows from our understanding of this. Yes, it's very hard to see masses of people suffer and not be able to put a stop to this suffering, right at the time; and, yes, we should organize the masses to fight back against their oppression and the ways in which this system causes them to suffer; but if we really understand where "the antibiotics" are and who's hoarding and monopolizing them and turning them into machinery for profit, into capital, and what it is that's preventing the masses of people from getting to those antibiotics, then our responsibility is to lead the masses to rise up and seize those things and distribute them among themselves.

Now, let me emphasize again: I can and do admire the morality of people who want to alleviate suffering (and who may not see beyond that). We should in no way denigrate or put down these people—people who do things like put water in the desert for immigrants crossing from Mexico—we should admire them and we should unite with them. But that cannot provide the fundamental solution to that particular problem, of the suffering of these immigrants and what drives them to leave their homelands in the first place, nor can it eliminate all the other ways in which masses of people, throughout the world, are oppressed and caused to suffer. Or, again, while I admire the people who volunteer with things like Doctors Without Borders, if they were to say, "this is the most anybody can do, there's nothing more you can do," we would have to engage in principled but very sharp struggle with them, even while uniting with them and admiring their spirit, because it is objectively *not* true that this is all that can, or should, be done—and it is *harmful* to the masses of people to say that this is all that can be done.

In fundamental and strategic terms, it is necessary to choose where the weight and the essence of your efforts is going to go: into fighting the effects and the symptoms, or getting to the cause and uprooting and getting rid of that cause? And that's why you become a revolutionary—when you realize that you have to seek the full solution to this, or else the suffering is going to continue, and get worse. That's one of the main things that impels people toward revolution, even before they understand, scientifically, all the complexity of what revolution means and what it requires. And, as you become a communist and you increasingly look at the whole world, and not just the part of the world that you are immediately situated in, you see that the whole world has to change, that all oppression and exploitation has to be uprooted, everywhere, so that it can no longer exist anywhere.

So we have to be on a mission to liberate those antibiotics, and not get diverted into thinking that the most and the highest good we can do is trying to lessen the misery, to mitigate the symptoms, rather than getting to the cause and bringing about a real and lasting cure. The question of reform vs. revolution is not some petty notion of "our thing" vs. somebody else's "thing"—it is a matter of what is really required to eliminate the horrendous suffering to which the great majority of humanity is subjected, day after day, and what kind of world is possible.

Nor are we revolutionaries because it's a "fashionable" thing to do—right now, in fact, it's not very fashionable at all. Back in the '60s, among certain sections of the people, Black people and others, being a revolutionary was a "legitimate avocation": *What do you do? I'm a doctor. What do you do? I'm a basketball player. What do you do? I'm a revolutionary.* Legitimate avocation. I was talking to another veteran comrade about this, and they pointed out that, in a certain sense, it was easier in those days to be a revolutionary because you had a lot of "social approbation"—there was a lot of approval coming from significant sections of society for being a revolutionary. Right now you don't get that much "social approbation" for being a revolutionary, and in particular a revolutionary *communist*. [*laughter*] "What the fuck, you crazy?!" [*laughter*] That's a lot of what you get, as you know. Or you get more theoretically developed arguments about why it's hopeless or a bad idea, or a disaster, or a nightmare. Well, we aren't doing this because we're seeking social approbation. It's good in one sense if you have that—in the sense that it reflects favorable elements in society, in terms of how people are viewing the question of radical change—but we're not doing what we're doing in order to get "social approbation," and we're not relying on such "social approbation" for what we're doing. If there isn't "social approbation," we have to create it—not so people will "approve" of what we're doing, in some more narrow or personal sense, but because we need to transform people's understanding of reality and therefore the way they act in terms of transforming reality.

So this is a fundamental question of orientation, but that orientation is not just: revolution, it's more righteous. "Reform, that sounds kind of paltry;

revolutionary, that's more righteous." [*laughter*] No, that's not the heart of the matter. It's very righteous to be in Doctors Without Borders. But the essential thing is that revolution corresponds to reality, it corresponds to what's needed to resolve the contradictions that have been spoken to repeatedly in this talk—the fundamental contradiction of capitalism and other contradictions bound up with that, and all the effects of this in the world—to resolve these contradictions in the interests of the masses of people. That's why we're revolutionaries—and a certain kind of revolutionaries—*communist* revolutionaries. Because that's the only kind of revolution that can do what needs to be done, what cries out to be done. So what we do has to proceed from that, in terms of our fundamental orientation.

CHAPTER 2
A WHOLE NEW –
AND FAR BETTER – WORLD

#1

Communism: A Whole New World and the Emancipation of All Humanity – Not "The Last Shall Be First, and The First Shall Be Last"

Title of one of the 7 Talks by Bob Avakian, 2006

#2

Marx said about the future world, the world of communism, that it will seem as ridiculous and outrageous for one part of society to privately own the land, and everything that goes along with that, as it now seems for one human being to own another.

Communism will mean that we have reached the point where the very idea that the way society should advance is for a few to benefit and then to proclaim that to be in the general interest of the society, where that idea will seem so ridiculous and outrageous that in a certain sense, to put it simply, it couldn't get a hearing.

"The Role of Dissent in a Vibrant Society,"
Observations on Art and Culture, Science and Philosophy, 2005
(quote originally published 2004)

#3

Now let's imagine, let's step out of this world that they keep us chained in. And let's imagine what this future can and will be like.

When we finally get to the final goal of communism, there won't be the relations of exploitation and oppression that are so commonplace and that mark all of society today and that we are told over and over again are just the natural order of things and the way things have to be. As Karl Marx pointed out, the communist revolution leads to what we Maoists call the "4 Alls"—that is, the abolition of all class differences among people. The abolition or the end to all the production or economic relations underlying these class differences and divisions among people. The ending of all the social relations that go along with these economic or production relations. Oppressive relations between men and women, between different nationalities, between people of different parts of the world, all that will be put an end to and moved beyond. And finally, the revolutionizing of all the ideas that go along with this whole way, this whole capitalist system, these whole social relations. In place of this, what will be the guiding principles in society consciously and voluntarily taken up by people... not forced on them, but consciously and voluntarily taken up as the basis for having abolished exploitation, oppression and inequality? In its place will be collective and cooperative principles aiming for the common good and at the same time, within that, individuals and individuality flourishing in a way that has never been possible before.

> *Revolution: Why It's Necessary, Why It's Possible, What It's All About, a film of a talk by Bob Avakian,* excerpt transcribed in *Revolution* #176, September 13, 2009. Film available at revolutiontalk.net and in a DVD set from RCP Publications.

#4

It is only possible today to conjecture, and to dream, about what expressions social contradictions will assume in the future communist society and how they will be resolved. How will the problem be approached of combining advanced productive forces, which require a significant degree of centralization, with decentralization and local initiative (whatever "local" means then)? How will the rearing of new generations of people—now carried out in atomized form, and through oppressive relations, in the family—be approached in communist society? How will attention be paid to developing specific areas of knowledge, or to concentrating on particular projects, without making these the "special preserve" of certain people? How will the contradiction be handled of enabling people to acquire all-around skills and knowledge and at the same time meeting the need for some specialization? What about the relation between people's individual initiatives and personal pursuits on the one hand, and their social responsibilities and contributions on the other? It seems that it will always be the case that, around any particular question, or controversy, there will be a group—and as a general rule a minority at first—that will have a more correct, advanced understanding, but how will this be utilized for the overall benefit while at the same time preventing groups from solidifying into "interest groups"? What will be the relations between different areas and regions—since there will no longer be different countries—and how will the contradictions between what might be called "local communities" and the higher associations, all the way up to the world level, be handled? What will it mean concretely that people are truly citizens of the world, particularly in terms of where they live, work, and so on—will they "rotate" from one area of the world to another? How will the question of linguistic and cultural diversity versus a world union of humanity be handled? And will people then, even with all their understanding of history, really be able to believe that a society such as we are imprisoned in now actually existed—let alone that it was declared to be eternal and the highest pinnacle humanity was capable of reaching? Again, these questions, and many, many more, can only be the object of speculation, and of dreaming, today; but even to pose such questions, and to attempt to visualize how

they might be addressed—in a society where class
divisions, social antagonism, and political domination
no longer exist—is itself tremendously liberating for
anyone without a vested interest in the present order.

Democracy: Can't We Do Better Than That?, 1986

#5

The first great step or great leap in the road to
communism is seizing power from the capitalists.
Without that none of this is possible. But seizing power
from them opens that way to making the advance to
communism.

Socialism is the new society established after the
seizure of power. Socialism is three things: a new
economic system, a new political system and a
transition to the final goal of communism. Let's talk
about what this will make possible right away, once
power has been seized. Let's talk about the whole
different nature of socialism as a society in which the
masses of people are digging up the old rotten and
putrid soil of capitalism and moving forward to the
goal of a communist world.

Revolution – a film of a talk by Bob Avakian,
excerpt transcribed in *Revolution* #176, September 13, 2009

#6

Let's talk about work and housing together. Look
at all these neighborhoods which under the rule of
the capitalist system have been allowed and even

encouraged to rot. Look at the youth and others just hanging out on the street corner with nothing to do or no way to do anything that doesn't get them into one kind of trouble or another. Imagine changing all that because now we have the power over society—we go to these youth and we say, "Here, we're going to give you training. We're going to give you education. We're going to bring you materials. We're going to enable you to go to work to build some beautiful housing and playgrounds and neighborhoods here for yourself and those who live here." Imagine if we said to them, you can not just work, you can be part of planning all this, you can be part of figuring out what should be done for the benefit of the people to make this society better and to contribute to making a whole different and radically better world. Imagine if for these youth, they could have a way, not just to make a living, building housing, hospitals, community centers and parks and other things people need, but at the same time, they could have the opportunity and the dignity of working together with people throughout society to build a whole better world. There's absolutely no reason why these things aren't possible except that we live under this system which makes them impossible.

Revolution – a film of a talk by Bob Avakian,
excerpt transcribed in *Revolution* #176, September 13, 2009

#7

Let's talk about education. Imagine kids who actually wanted to go to school! Imagine if they weren't degraded and insulted all the time and treated as if they couldn't possibly learn anything or have any important ideas. Imagine if the educational system actually told them the truth and helped them to understand about the world and history and nature and society. Imagine if it actually helped them to think critically, to challenge everything. Yes the teachers, and yes even the party and its leaders.

What if the educational system drew the kids in along with the teachers and staff and said this is a whole new society, a new world—what are your ideas about how this could all be done better? Imagine if the education combined practical things with theory so the things they were studying and learning, they would go out in society and talk to people who did those things. Or, instead of casting the old people off, like useless garbage, they invite the old people in to talk about the horrors of the old society and their experience, and what the new society means to them, and have them have an exchange with these kids in the schools. And have the students learn practical knowledge as well as studying theory, learning science and grappling with philosophy.

The same in science. Right now science often scares
people. It's intimidating. You're taught that you
can't possibly understand these things. That it's all
mysterious. It's not the scientists' fault. Or at least
not mainly. It's the kind of society we have and the
way in which they want people to be divided into
different classes, groups and castes so that some
people use their minds and other people can only use
their bodies or just waste away, or die fighting in a
war. Imagine if science were brought to everybody
and made the exciting thing it is for everybody.
Struggling to investigate and learn about the world
and the way it works and all the different things
both here on earth and in the far—what the religious
people call the heavens. Imagine if here in the
realm of science, the scientists got together with the
"ordinary people"—with the students in the schools,
with the workers in workplaces, and talked to them
about science, drew them into scientific experiments
and investigation, got their ideas and found out the
questions they wanted to know about the world,
then worked out ways of people uniting together and
cooperating to develop experiments and investigation
in science that pursued these things. Imagine if
science, like education and all these other parts of
society, actually were serving to transform a society
to get rid of oppression, exploitation and inequality

and to help the people throughout the world wage a revolutionary struggle to do the same.

Revolution – a film of a talk by Bob Avakian,
excerpt transcribed in *Revolution* #176, September 13, 2009

#8

Let's imagine if we had a whole different art and culture. Come on, enough of this "bitches and ho's" and SWAT teams kicking down doors. Enough of this "get low" bullshit. And how come it's always the women that have to get low? We already have a situation where the masses of women and the masses of people are pushed down and held down low enough already. It's time for us to get up and get on up.

Imagine if we had a society where there was culture—yes it was lively and full of creativity and energy and yes rhythm and excitement, but at the same time, instead of degrading people, lifted us up. Imagine if it gave us a vision and a reality of what it means to make a whole different society and a whole different kind of world. Imagine if it laid out the problems for people in making this kind of world and challenged them to take up these problems. Imagine if art and culture too—movies, songs, television, everything—challenged people to think critically, to look at things differently, to see things in a different light, but all pointing toward how can we make a better world.

Imagine if the people who created art and culture were not just a handful of people but all of the masses of people, with all their creative energy unleashed, and the time were made for them to do that, and for them to join with people who are more full-time workers and creators in the realm of art and culture to bring forward something new that would challenge people, that would make them think in different ways, that would make them be able to see things critically and from a different angle, and would help them to be uplifted and help them to see their unity with each other and with people throughout the world in putting an end to all the horrors that we're taught are just the natural order of things. Imagine all that.

Revolution – a film of a talk by Bob Avakian,
excerpt transcribed in *Revolution* #176, September 13, 2009

#9

This is not a fantasy. These are the things that have been done in the socialist societies that have existed—or they're the things that, on the basis of that experience, we have summed up and are learning more deeply need to be done. This is all possible. It's not some pipe dream. This is what happens when the masses of people rise up and take control over society and this is what waits to be done.

Revolution – a film of a talk by Bob Avakian,
excerpt transcribed in *Revolution* #176, September 13, 2009

#10

It is **right** to want state power. It is **necessary** to want state power. State power is a **good** thing— state power is a **great** thing—in the hands of the right people, the right class, in the service of the right things: bringing about an end to exploitation, oppression, and social inequality and bringing into being a world, a communist world, in which human beings can flourish in new and greater ways than ever before.

"Views on Socialism and Communism: A Radically New Kind of State, A Radically Different and Far Greater Vision of Freedom," *Revolution* #37, March 5, 2006

#11

Put the advance of the world revolution above everything, even above the advance of the revolution in the particular country—build the socialist state as above all a base area for the world revolution.

"A Final Note," *Revolution* magazine, Fall 1990

#12

The achievement of [the necessary conditions for communism] must take place on a world scale, through a long and tortuous process of revolutionary transformation in which there will be uneven development, the seizure of power in different countries at different times, and a complex dialectical

interplay between the revolutionary struggles and
the revolutionization of society in these different
countries...[a dialectical relation] in which the world
arena is fundamentally and ultimately decisive while
the mutually interacting and mutually supporting
struggles of the proletarians in different countries
constitute the key link in fundamentally changing the
world as a whole.

> Originally appeared in *Phony Communism Is Dead...Long Live Real
> Communism!* 1992 (Second Edition, 2004). Cited in "Revolution
> and A Radically New World: Contending 'Universalisms' and
> Communist Internationalism," *Revolution* #157, February 22, 2009

#13

It is not simply a matter—nor is the essence of the
matter—that, as Lenin put it, socialism, with the
dictatorship of the proletariat, is a million times
more democratic, for the masses of people, than
capitalism, with its dictatorship of the <u>bourgeoisie</u>.
Beyond that, the socialist system embodies and
involves—and <u>must</u> embody and involve, if it is in
fact to carry forward the transition to communism—<u>a
radically different process</u>, which is emancipating in
a <u>qualitatively different and greater way</u>.

> *Birds Cannot Give Birth to Crocodiles,*
> *But Humanity Can Soar Beyond the Horizon* – Part 1:
> "Revolution and the State," *Revolution*, 2011

#14

So, yes, there must be in socialist society—and in
communist society—a recognition of the importance
of individual conscience, and of the right, and
fundamentally of the need, for people to create various
works of literature and art which embody and give life to
different particular ways of "coming at" reality (or a part
of reality), different modes of "individual expression."
There is an important role for that, and there must
be a broad scope for that—both as something that's
important in itself and also, in a deeper sense, as part of
the overall process of coming to understand the world
in increasingly richer ways and continuing to transform
it in accordance with the largest interests of humanity.
All this is part of the objective of advancing to—and
then continuing to advance in—the radically new era of
communism. But this is very different from—and will
be much more fully expressed the more that it moves
beyond—notions of individual conscience and individual
creativity as *private property*—which inevitably means
in conflict and competition with other embodiments of
private property.

Communism and Jeffersonian Democracy, 2008

#15

There would not be a General Motors in socialist
society, and there would also not be an FBI or an

LAPD. Those kinds of institutions would be abolished and—unless they agreed to abolish themselves voluntarily—they would have to be forcefully abolished under a future dictatorship of the proletariat. Maybe they would be given 24 hours to disband!... but disbanded they would have to be. There would be revolutionary institutions in place of those old, oppressive and reactionary institutions...and, yes, that is what we're building for—aiming for the time when there is a qualitative change in the objective situation, when a revolutionary situation and a revolutionary people in the millions and millions have been brought into being. And when that revolution is made, when a new, revolutionary state power is brought into being, there would not just be a new army, but that new army would be <u>guided by very different principles</u>. There would be a culture in that army, but it would definitely not be (as in the hymn of the imperialist Marine Corps): "From the halls of Montezuma to the shores of Tripoli"—that's just not going to be what guides the new state apparatus! No more General Motors and no more Marines. The principles we're talking about here, and the reason we're going out to win people to be emancipators of humanity, is that they're going to be the actual backbone of the new state.

"There <u>Is No</u> 'Permanent Necessity' for Things To Be This Way, A Radically Different and Better World <u>Can</u> Be Brought Into Being Through Revolution," *Revolution* #198, April 11, 2010

#16

Editor's note: Tyisha Miller was a 19-year-old African-American woman shot dead by Riverside, California police in 1998. Miller had been passed out in her car, resulting from a seizure, when police claimed that she suddenly awoke and had a gun; they fired 23 times at her, hitting her at least 12 times, and murdering her. Bob Avakian addressed this.

If you can't handle this situation differently than this, then get the fuck out of the way. Not only out of the way of this situation, but get off the earth. Get out of the way of the masses of people. Because, you know, we could have handled this situation any number of ways that would have resulted in a much better outcome. And frankly, if we had state power and we were faced with a similar situation, we would sooner have one of our own people's police killed than go wantonly murder one of the masses. That's what you're supposed to do if you're actually trying to be a servant of the people. You go there and you put your own life on the line, rather than just wantonly murder one of the people. Fuck all this "serve and protect" bullshit! If they were there to serve and protect, they would have found any way but the way they did it to handle this scene. They could have and would have found a solution that was much better than this. This is the way the proletariat, when it's been in power has handled—and would again handle—this kind of thing, valuing the lives of the masses of people. As opposed to the bourgeoisie in power, where the role of *their* police is to terrorize the masses, including wantonly murdering them, murdering them without provocation, without necessity, because exactly the more arbitrary the terror is, the more broadly it affects the masses. And that's one of the reasons why they like to engage in, and have as one of their main functions to engage in, wanton and arbitrary terror against the masses of people.

"Putting Forward Our Line in a Bold, Moving, Compelling Way," *Revolutionary Worker* #1177, December 1, 2002

#17

The aim of the class-conscious proletariat is to achieve the unity of the masses of people, on a revolutionary basis. And, all other things being equal, the proletariat generally favors the establishment of a unified socialist state in the largest possible territory. This is our objective in carrying out the struggle to overthrow the present exploitative rule of capital and to establish the revolutionary rule of the proletariat; and this is consistent with and is guided by our final objective of achieving communism on a worldwide basis.

But the point is exactly this: The revolutionary unity of the masses of different nationalities and the new, revolutionary socialist state must embody the equality of peoples. The unification of this state must be the voluntary act of the masses of people of all different nationalities. It cannot be based on and held together by one nationality dominating others, reproducing the same old inequality—or inequality in some new forms—between different peoples and in particular the domination of the European-American nation over other peoples. And we must keep clearly in mind that the new socialist society that will be brought into being through the overthrow of the present oppressive system will have to deal with the consequences and effects of the whole historical development of the capitalist-imperialist system in the U.S., where white supremacy has been built into its fundamental structures and ruling institutions and dominant culture.

This will have to be taken into account in many different ways, including in terms of people "wanting to live around other people of their race," within the new socialist society. In correctly handling this, it will be necessary and decisive to consistently apply the basic standard of supporting and promoting those things that help to overcome the whole history and legacy of national oppression in the U.S., while opposing those things that set back the struggle against white supremacy.

> From a four-part series: "The Oppression of Black People and the Revolutionary Struggle to End All Oppression," *Revolution*, February 2007

#18

Editor's note: Here Bob Avakian recalls his visit to socialist China in 1971, before the death of Mao Tsetung and the restoration of capitalism in that country.

There were all these really exciting and uplifting things. We felt the whole spirit of "serve the people" that was popularized throughout the society, and we saw living examples of revolutionary transformations. We'd come upon situations where the men and women would be engaging in friendly competition to do things like sweeping up in the house. Again, you think about China coming from a feudal society less than twenty-five years before that, and here you had these big changes in the relations between men and women. Even though this was a small example, in a sense—and even though, of course, many backward ideas and practices still persisted and were still contending with these more advanced things—this friendly competition captured both the "serve the people" spirit and the pervasiveness of the changes that were going on between men and women.

We would have discussions in factories with workers who were reading Engels' *Anti-Dühring*, which is a major theoretical work of Marxism, and who were reading other works of Marxist philosophy and debating all these big questions. In a number of factories we talked to members of what they called "three-in-one leadership committees," or revolutionary committees, in which party members and administrative personnel from the factory, together with workers selected from the shop floor, made up the committee that led the whole factory. This was a very exciting development and a whole new thing even in the history of socialism, let alone in contrast with what goes on in capitalist society.

We visited a hospital and saw how, as a result of the Cultural Revolution, they had actually instituted the practice of doing anesthesia with acupuncture. Our delegation went to three or four operations— for things like stomach cancer—and it was very advanced medical practice, but they were also integrating traditional practices from Chinese culture into an overall system of medicine which for the first time was geared toward serving the ordinary people, and as a result of the Cultural Revolution was being spread throughout the countryside, where the vast majority of Chinese people lived.

We talked to people on cultural teams. China was still a backward country, it was only a few decades from feudalism and domination by imperialism—a society where, for generations and centuries, the masses of people in the countryside were barely hanging on and millions were regularly starving, even in the "better" years. Things like movies and other cultural productions were known in the cities, although even those were overwhelmingly for the elite, well-to-do

Chinese and foreigners, and virtually none of this existed in the countryside, before the revolution. We saw people who, on bicycles, were taking movie projectors to spread revolutionary culture, the culture of the new socialist society, in the countryside.

We saw truly wondrous things.

From Ike to Mao and Beyond: My Journey from Mainstream America to Revolutionary Communist, A Memoir by Bob Avakian, 2005

#19

It is easy to have a society where a privileged intellectual elite has considerable freedom to grapple with ideas—as long as they stay within certain confines and don't fundamentally challenge the existing order....

The hard thing is turning all of this upside down without stifling the critical spirit, the wrangling over ideas and theories and so on. Because we have also seen from history that it might be quite easy to institute a kind of monolithic system where only a few ideas are allowed to be debated out and where there is not real critical thinking and dissent. And we have seen that, to the degree that this is a tendency in socialist society, it works against socialism, against the revolutionary transformation of society, against the advance to communism.

"The End of a Stage – The Beginning of a New Stage," *Revolution* magazine, Fall 1990

#20

In socialist society, there needs to be struggle, and criticism/self-criticism, but there also needs to be "air" for people to breathe, room for them to disagree, allowance for them to come to the truths that Marxism reveals in their own way—and allowance for Marxism itself to breathe and grow, to discard outmoded concepts and analyses and to deepen its reflection of reality, as the liberating science it is, in opposition to suffocating religious dogma.

"The End of a Stage – The Beginning of a New Stage"

#21

In socialist society we should not act as if the central authority is all-knowing and as if things will be fine if it relies on its authority to get masses to go along with things, rather than relying on the masses to grasp their own interests and act accordingly, with leadership and through lively, vigorous debate and struggle. We cannot rely on such authority when we don't have it, in the old society, and we should not try to rely on it when we do have it in the new society—or it won't last long either.

"The End of a Stage – The Beginning of a New Stage"

#22

Does this mean that I am calling for liberalism and bourgeois democracy after all—that I am opposing the dictatorship of the proletariat? No. I am not

talking about *whether* the proletariat should exercise
dictatorship but *how* it should exercise it. Everything
I'm talking about must be carried out in the context that
the proletariat has seized power and has consolidated
its rule, that the proletariat, with the leadership of its
vanguard party, is running society and is in overall
control of not only the economy but politics, the media,
culture, and so on. But dictatorship and control by the
proletariat need not mean, and should not mean, that
no opposition is allowed....

The masses increasingly strengthening their mastery
over society and their ability to transform it in their
interests has everything to do with the points I am
stressing here about dissent, about unity and diversity,
about contradiction and struggle.

"The End of a Stage – The Beginning of a New Stage"

#23

Your attitude towards intellectuals has to do with
the philosophical question of what you think we're
trying to do, and what is it the proletariat represents.
What is the "godlike position of the proletariat,"
as I referred to it in *Strategic Questions*? On one
level, you're sort of sitting on a hill watching this
procession go by of the development of humanity.
Some of it you can see more dimly and some more
clearly—you look at this whole sweep and then at a
certain point this group called the proletariat emerges

from within this set of social relations that can take
it to a particular place, to a whole different world.
But you shouldn't reify the proletariat. Yes, it's made
up of real people, but it's not a matter of individual
proletarians but of the proletariat as a class, of its
position in society and of where its interests lie, in
the most fundamental sense, as a class. On another
level, looking at the sweep of history, you see the role
of intellectuals as well. Are they basically making
trouble for us? This is how some people see it—and
this has been a definite tendency, and real problem,
in the history of our movement.

But from the standpoint of a sweeping view of
history, you look at this a different way. For example,
there is this physicist Brian Greene who has written
some books popularizing questions of physics, and
he speaks to this big contradiction the physicists
can't yet resolve between relativity and quantum
mechanics, so the question they're facing is: how do
you get the next level of synthesis? What do we think
of that—is that a big waste of time unless we can use
that narrowly?...[Of course] people like this, people
in these fields generally, need to be struggled with—
but in a good way. If we were working in the right
way in these spheres we'd be having a lot of good
struggle with people around all kinds of questions,
including questions arising in their work, but first of

all we would be seriously engaging the work they are
doing and the questions they are wrestling with. We
would do this in a different way than it's often been
done in the history of our movement. Is it important
for what we're trying to accomplish, or should
be trying to accomplish, whether these physicists
understand more about the world? Yes. Do they need
"loose reins" to accomplish this? Yes. Do we need to
struggle with them? Yes. Do we need to have them
come down and learn from the masses? Yes. But
there is a legitimate part to the point that Bill Martin
has made, in an introduction to a book that will
be coming out soon*—consisting of a conversation
between him and me—the point that, yes, there are
problems of intellectuals getting isolated in their
ivory towers but at the same time there is a definite
need for intellectuals to have the right atmosphere
and space in which to do their work.

> "Bob Avakian in a Discussion with Comrades
> on Epistemology: On Knowing and Changing the World,"
> *Observations on Art and Culture, Science and Philosophy*, 2005

* This conversation between Bob Avakian and Bill Martin has
been published as the book *Marxism and the Call of the Future,
Conversations on Ethics, History, and Politics.*

#24

We should not only allow but even encourage
oppositional politics under the dictatorship of the
proletariat, because we have to conceive of this process

not as a neat and orderly one but as a very tumultuous one—and a volatile and chaotic one at times—through which a lot of things get brought forward and thrashed out by the masses. Now, this doesn't mean that we can just turn power back over to the bourgeoisie indirectly or inadvertently by "loosening the reins" so much that there's no core that's driving the society forward to where it needs to go and is leading the masses of people to ever more consciously and voluntarily strive for those things. But that shouldn't be seen as like an engine on a track that's going straight ahead. It's a much more tumultuous and tortuous process where a lot of different things are going to get into the mix and a lot of different contradictions are going to be wrestled over, and a lot of different ideas are going to be brought forward about how to do that, and where increasingly the masses are being relied on and involved consciously in the process of thrashing these things out themselves.

Dictatorship and Democracy, and the Socialist Transition to Communism, Revolutionary Worker #1257, October 31, 2004

#25

This brings up one very important factor in all this: the positive side of unresolved contradictions under socialism—the bringing to the fore of driving forces for revolutionary transformation in the socialist stage—forces on the cutting edge of contradictions that are coming to the fore as decisive questions in

terms of whether society will be moved forward or
dragged backward. A very important aspect of all this
is the woman question, the struggle for the complete
emancipation of women. This will be a decisive
question giving rise to crucial struggle throughout the
socialist period.

Along with this are other divisions and inequalities left
over from the old society....Unleashing all these forces
[related to these unresolved contradictions in socialist
society] to speak out, rally forces, raise criticism, and
rise in rebellion can be risky and messy. But such mass
upheaval is no less essential under socialism than it is
under capitalism. And certainly this is not something
communists should fear!

                  "The End of a Stage – The Beginning of a New Stage"

#26

In order to handle this correctly, there are a couple
principles that I think are very important. One was
actually articulated for me in a conversation that
I had not long ago with a spoken word artist and
poet. I was laying out to him how I saw socialist
society and some of the same points that I'm making
here about how we have to hang onto power and
keep things going in a forward direction toward
communism, while on the other hand there is a need
for a lot of experimentation in the arts, a lot of critical
thinking that needs to go on in the sciences and all

these different spheres, and you have to let people take the ball and run with it, and not supervise them at every point on everything they do. And I asked him, for example: could you write your poetry if every step of the way there was a party cadre there looking over your shoulder, examining what you are writing. He said "no way."

Then, as we discussed this for a while, he came up with what I thought was a very good formulation. He said, "It sounds to me like what you are talking about is 'a solid core with a lot of elasticity.'" And I said "yeah, you've really hit on something there," because that was exactly what I was trying to give voice to—that you have to have a solid core that firmly grasps and is committed to the strategic objectives and aims and process of the struggle for communism. If you let go of that you are just giving everything back to the capitalists in one form or another, with all the horrors that means. At the same time, if you don't allow for a lot of diversity and people running in all kinds of directions with things, then not only are people going to be building up tremendous resentment against you, but you are also not going to have the rich kind of process out of which the greatest truth and ability to transform reality will emerge.

Dictatorship and Democracy, and the Socialist Transition to Communism, Revolutionary Worker #1257, October 31, 2004

#27

At a talk I gave, years ago now, someone asked:
"How would you do better than the Soviet Union or
China under Mao?" One of the things I said to him
is: "I don't believe in tailing people because they're
oppressed—we need emancipators of humanity."
When you are in a qualitatively different situation
than what we have now—when the present system
has been swept aside and the new, socialist system has
been brought into being—there would have to be an
army, as the backbone of an actual state, that enforces
the new system, and that army would be made up of
very basic people in large part. But we have to train
them to understand that, as part of that, they are going
to have to be out there protecting the rights of people
who oppose this new system, and they are going to
have to defend the right of these people to raise this
opposition, while at the same time they would also
have to stop people who really are making attempts
to smash the state power we have. I said that this
will be a struggle with masses, but we have to bring
forward on every level people who have this kind of
understanding of what we're doing. The Constitution
of the new, socialist system is going to enumerate
the rights of people, and this state apparatus is going
to protect people's rights who don't agree, so long
as they don't actively and concretely organize to
overthrow that state apparatus. That is where the
Lenin point comes in: As long as there are classes, one

class is going to dictate, and "better me than you"—
that is, better the dictatorship of the proletariat than
the dictatorship of the bourgeoisie (capitalist class).
But what is that dictatorship of the proletariat?

BOTH aspects of this are important—solid core and
elasticity.

"There Is No 'Permanent Necessity' for Things To Be This Way"

#28

I have spoken before about the four objectives of the
solid core, in socialist society—namely: to maintain
power for the proletarian revolution; to expand
the solid core to the greatest extent possible at any
given time; to work to constantly narrow, and work
toward finally overcoming, the difference between
the solid core and the rest of society (this speaks to
"the withering away of the state"); and to foster the
maximum elasticity on the basis of the necessary solid
core at any given time. All four of these objectives
form a unity and are mutually interdependent and
mutually influence each other, one way or the other.
And, as I've said, even in communist society—
although in a radically different way—this same
principle will still apply, because it conforms to,
or is an expression of, the nature of reality and its
development through contradictory motion.

Making Revolution and Emancipating Humanity – Part 1:
"Beyond the Narrow Horizon of Bourgeois Right,"
Revolution #112, December 16, 2007

#29

The challenge is one of developing and applying the correct principles and methods so that all of this develops in such a way that it serves the advance toward communism, toward a communist world, so that socialist society is a vital and vibrant society in which masses of people are, in a great diversity of ways, increasingly wrangling with and engaging all kinds of questions having to do with the nature and direction of society; and, through all this, not only is political power maintained in a way that serves the fundamental interests and needs of the masses of the people and the world revolution, but the advance is carried forward toward the eventual abolition of state power altogether and the emergence of a community of freely associating human beings all over the world, a communist world where, to quote Mao, human beings consciously and voluntarily transform themselves and the objective world. And all this will be achieved through a wrenching process of struggle and wrangling, and not in some orderly, neat straight line way, and not with uniformity of opinion about everything all the time, by any means.

Dictatorship and Democracy, and the Socialist Transition to Communism, Revolutionary Worker #1257, October 31, 2004

#30

This takes us back to the very important point
from "The End of a Stage—The Beginning of a
New Stage" about unresolved contradictions under
socialism. What is said there is another way of
expressing the understanding that the struggle
for the complete emancipation of women will be a
crucial part of "the final revolution." In other words,
it will be a crucial component in propelling and
driving forward not only the revolutionary struggle
to overthrow the rule of capitalism-imperialism
but to continue the revolution, within the new,
socialist society itself, in order to advance on the
road toward the final aim of communism. The point
is that, among the unresolved contradictions which
will remain in socialist society, and which can be
a driving force propelling that revolution forward,
the continuing ways in which the emancipation
of women will need to be fought for and fought
through will be one of the most decisive aspects and
expressions of that.

Unresolved Contradictions, Driving Forces for Revolution – Part III:
"The New Synthesis and the Woman Question: The Emancipation
of Women and the Communist Revolution – Further Leaps and
Radical Ruptures," *Revolution* #197, April 4, 2010

#31

Editor's note: Over the past several decades, Bob Avakian has been developing a new synthesis of communism. Here he speaks to essential elements of this new synthesis.

This new synthesis involves a recasting and recombining of the positive aspects of the experience so far of the communist movement and of socialist society, while learning from the negative aspects of this experience, in the philosophical and ideological as well as the political dimensions, so as to have a more deeply and firmly rooted scientific orientation, method and approach with regard not only to making revolution and seizing power but then, yes, to meeting the material requirements of society and the needs of the masses of people, in an increasingly expanding way, in socialist society—overcoming the deep scars of the past and continuing the revolutionary transformation of society, while at the same time actively supporting the world revolutionary struggle and acting on the recognition that the world arena and the world struggle are most fundamental and important, in an overall sense—*together with* opening up qualitatively more space to give expression to the intellectual and cultural needs of the people, broadly understood, and enabling a more diverse and rich process of exploration and experimentation in the realms of science, art and culture, and intellectual life overall, with increasing scope for the contention of different ideas and schools of thought and for individual initiative and creativity and protection of individual rights, including space for individuals to interact in "civil society" independently of the state—all within an overall cooperative and collective framework and at the same time as state power is maintained and further developed as a *revolutionary* state power serving the interests of the proletarian revolution, in the particular country and worldwide, with this state being the leading and central element in the economy and in the overall direction of society, while the state itself is being continually transformed into something radically different from all previous states, as a crucial part of the advance toward the eventual abolition of the state with the achievement of communism on a world scale.

Making Revolution and Emancipating Humanity – Part 1,
Revolution #112, December 16, 2007

#32

We should not underestimate the potential of [the new synthesis] as a source of hope and of daring on a solid scientific foundation. In the 1960s, when the Black Panther Party emerged on the scene, Eldridge Cleaver made the pungent observation that the old revisionist Communist Party had "ideologized" revolution off the scene, but the Panthers had "ideologized" it back on the scene. In the present period in the U.S., revolution has once more been "ideologized" off the scene. And in the world as a whole, to a very large degree, revolution aiming for communism and the vision of a communist world— this has been "ideologized" off the scene—and with it the only road that actually represents the possibility of a radically different and far better world, in the real world, one that people really would want to live in and would really thrive in. The new synthesis has *objectively* "ideologized" this back on the scene once more, on a higher level and in a potentially very powerful way.

But what will be done with this? Will it become a powerful political as well as ideological force? It is up to us to take this out everywhere—very, very boldly and with substance, linking it with the widespread, if still largely latent, desire for another way, for another world—and engage ever growing numbers of people with this new synthesis in a good, lively and living way.

Making Revolution and Emancipating Humanity – Part 1,
Revolution #112, December 16, 2007

Supplement

Three Alternative Worlds

Editor's note: The following is from "Three Alternative Worlds" in Bob Avakian's 2005 book *Observations on Art and Culture, Science and Philosophy.*

As the world exists today and as people seek to change it, and particularly in terms of the socialist transformation of society, as I see it there are basically three alternatives that are possible. One is the world as it is. Enough said about that. [*laughter*]

The second one is in a certain sense, almost literally and mechanically, turning the world upside down. In other words, people who are now exploited will no longer be exploited in the same way, people who now rule this society will be prevented from ruling or influencing society in a significant way. The basic economic structure of society will change, some of the social relations will change, and some of the forms of political rule will change, and some of the forms of culture and ideology will change, but fundamentally the masses of people will not be increasingly and in one leap after another drawn into the process of really transforming society. This is really a vision of a revisionist society. If you think back to the days of the Soviet Union, when it had become a revisionist society, capitalist and imperialist in essence, but still socialist in name, when they would be chided for their alleged or real violations of people's rights, they would often answer, "Who are you in the West to be talking about the violation of human rights—look at all the people in your society who are unemployed, what more basic human right is there than to have a job?"

Well, did they have a point? Yes, up to a point. But fundamentally what they were putting forward, the vision of society that they were projecting, was a social welfare kind of society in which fundamentally the role of the masses of people is no different than it is under the classical form of capitalism. The answer about the rights of the people cannot be reduced to the right to have a job and earn an income, as basic as that is. There is the question of are we really going to transform society so that in every respect, not only economically but socially, politically, ideologically, and culturally, it really is superior to capitalist society. A society that not only meets the needs of the masses of people, but really is characterized increasingly by the conscious expression and initiative of the masses of people.

This is a more fundamental transformation than simply a kind of social welfare, socialist in name but really capitalist in essence society, where the role of the masses of people is still largely reduced to being producers of wealth, but not people who thrash out all the larger questions of affairs of state, the direction of society, culture, philosophy, science, the arts, and so on. The revisionist model is a narrow, economist view of socialism. It reduces the people, in their activity, to simply the economic sphere of society, and in a limited way at that—simply their social welfare with regard to the economy. It doesn't even think about transforming the world outlook of the people as they in turn change the world around them.

And you cannot have a new society and a new world with the same outlook that people are indoctrinated and inculcated with in this society. You cannot have a real revolutionary transformation of society and abolition of unequal social as well as economic relations and political relations if people still approach the world in the way in which they're conditioned and limited and constrained to approach it now. How can the masses of people really take up the task of consciously changing the world if their outlook and their approach to the world remains what it is under this system? It's impossible, and this situation will simply reproduce the great inequalities in every sphere of society that I've been talking about.

The third alternative is a real radical rupture. Marx and Engels said in the Communist Manifesto that the communist revolution represents a radical rupture with traditional property relations and with traditional ideas. And the one is not possible without the other. They are mutually reinforcing, one way or the other.

If you have a society in which the fundamental role of women is to be breeders of children, how can you have a society in which there is equality between men and women? You cannot. And if you don't attack and uproot the traditions, the morals, and so on, that reinforce that role, how can you transform the relations between men and women and abolish the deep-seated inequalities that are bound up with the whole division of society into oppressors and oppressed, exploiters and exploited? You cannot.

So the third alternative is a real radical rupture in every sphere, a radically different synthesis, to put it that way. Or to put it another way, it's a society and a world that the great majority of people would actually want to live in. One in which not only do they not have to worry about where their next meal is coming from, or if they get sick whether they're going to be told that they can't have health care because they can't pay for it, as important as that is; but one in which they are actually taking up, wrangling with, and increasingly making their own province all the different spheres of society.

Achieving that kind of a society, and that kind of a world, is a very profound challenge. It's much more profound than simply changing a few forms of ownership of the economy and making sure that, on that basis, people's social welfare is taken care of, but you still have people who are taking care of that *for* the masses of people; and all the spheres of science, the arts, philosophy and all the rest are basically the province of a few. And the political decision-making process remains the province of a few.

To really leap beyond that is a tremendous and world-historic struggle that we've been embarked on since the Russian revolution (not counting the very short-lived and limited experience of the Paris Commune)—and in which we reached the high point with the Chinese revolution and in particular the Cultural Revolution—but from which we've been thrown back temporarily.

So we need to make a further leap on the basis of summing up very deeply all that experience. There are some very real and vexing problems that we have to confront and advance through in order to draw from the best of the past, but go further and do even better in the future.

CHAPTER 3
MAKING REVOLUTION

#1

Let's get down to basics: *We need a revolution. Anything else, in the final analysis, is bullshit.*

Now, that doesn't mean we don't unite with people in all sorts of struggles short of revolution. We definitely need to do that. But the proffering of any other solution to these monumental and monstrous problems and outrages is ridiculous, frankly. And we need to be taking the offensive and mobilizing increasing numbers of masses to cut through this shit and bring to the fore what really is the solution to this, and to answer the questions and, yes, the accusations that come forth in response to this, while deepening our scientific basis for being able to do this. And the point is: not only do *we* need to be doing this, but we need to be bringing forward, unleashing and leading, and enabling increasing numbers of the *masses* to do this. They need to be inspired, not just with a general idea of revolution, but with a deepening understanding, a scientific grounding, as to why and how revolution really *is* the answer to all of this.

Making Revolution and Emancipating Humanity – Part 2:
"Everything We're Doing Is About Revolution,"
Revolution #114, December 30, 2007

#2

There is nothing more *un*realistic than the idea of reforming this system into something that would come anywhere near being in the interests of the great majority of people and ultimately of humanity as a whole.

Making Revolution and Emancipating Humanity – Part 2,
Revolution #114, December 30, 2007

#3

It is important first to make clear what, in basic terms, we mean when we say the goal is revolution, and in particular communist revolution. Revolution is not some kind of change in style, or a change in attitude, nor is it merely a change in certain relations within a society which remains fundamentally the same. Revolution means nothing less than the defeat and dismantling of the existing, oppressive state, serving the capitalist-imperialist system—and in particular its institutions of organized violence and repression, including its armed forces, police, courts, prisons, bureaucracies and administrative power—and the replacement of those reactionary institutions, those concentrations of reactionary coercion and violence, with revolutionary organs of political power, and other revolutionary institutions and governmental structures, whose basis has been laid through the whole process of building the movement for revolution, and then carrying out the seizure of power, when the conditions for that have been brought into being—which in a country like the U.S. would require a qualitative change in the objective situation, resulting in a deep-going crisis in society, and the emergence of a revolutionary people in the millions and millions, who have the leadership of a revolutionary communist vanguard and are conscious of the need for revolutionary change and determined to fight for it.

As I emphasized earlier in this talk, the seizure of power and radical change in the dominant institutions of society, when the conditions for this have been brought into being, makes possible further radical change throughout society—in the economy and economic relations, the social relations, and the politics, ideology and culture prevailing in society. The final aim of this revolution is communism, which means and requires the abolition of all relations of exploitation and oppression and all destructive antagonistic conflicts among human beings, throughout the world. Understood in this light, the seizure of power, in a particular country, is crucial and decisive, and opens the door to further radical change, and to strengthening and further advancing the revolutionary struggle throughout the world; but, at the same time, as crucial and decisive as that is, it is only the first step—or first great leap—in an overall struggle which must continue toward the final goal of this revolution: a radically new, communist world.

Birds Cannot Give Birth to Crocodiles,
But Humanity Can Soar Beyond the Horizon – Part 2:
"Building the Movement for Revolution," *Revolution,* 2011

#4

One of the more important statements in the Manifesto
from our Party (*Communism: The Beginning of a
New Stage*) is the quote from Marx: "Once the inner
connection is grasped, all theoretical belief in the
permanent necessity of existing conditions breaks
down before their collapse in practice." This is not just
a matter of abstract theory—it has a broader effect. That
belief weighs heavily on people who don't like the way
things are—they are weighed down by a belief in the
"permanent necessity of existing conditions." Over and
over we are confronted by the fact that people can't see
beyond the way things are now....

A big part of transforming the people is, yes, a different
consciousness and morality, but also people seeing
the breakdown in their own understanding of the
"permanent necessity of existing conditions" and the
possibility of a whole different thing. This is related
again to how we talk to people: we ARE BUILDING a
movement for revolution—*not* asking them: "Would
it be a good idea to have a revolution?"—after which
they give all the reasons why it wouldn't, or why we
can't, and that sets the tone and conditions for what
follows. No, we don't ignore those questions—we talk
with people about them, but by saying, "okay, those
are points and we have thought about them and have
answers we can get into—but we ARE BUILDING

a movement for revolution and this is what that revolution will look like, and this is how everything we are doing is contributing to this revolution."

"There Is No 'Permanent Necessity' for Things To Be This Way, A Radically Different and Better World Can Be Brought Into Being Through Revolution," *Revolution* #198, April 11, 2010

#5

So this is what Marx discovered: You have highly socialized production, but very privatized appropriation by a small class of people called capitalists. But in that contradiction lies the basis for the overthrow of the system, as that class that carries out socialized production becomes conscious of this contradiction and of all of its consequences, and rises up and rallies its allies, as it is led by a vanguard party that brings it the consciousness to do this, and it eventually overthrows the system and resolves this contradiction through a whole long complex process whereby, step by step, it socializes the appropriation of what is socially produced and distributes it increasingly according to the needs of the people, not according to the dictates of the accumulation of private capital.

Dictatorship and Democracy, and the Socialist Transition to Communism, Revolutionary Worker #1252, September 19, 2004

#6

If you conceive of revolution as someday the world is somehow going to be radically different and at that point we will do something to radically change it...no,

that won't happen—but that's *not* what we're doing. We
have to elevate our sights and lead consistently with the
understanding that the world does NOT have to be this
way, and we ARE building a movement for revolution.

"There <u>Is No</u> 'Permanent Necessity' for Things To Be This Way"

#7

We need to give people a really living sense of what
we mean by "hastening while awaiting" the emergence
of a revolutionary situation. And this is linked to the
point that what we're doing is building a movement for
revolution and letting people know what we think that
revolution would look like.

"There <u>Is No</u> 'Permanent Necessity' for Things To Be This Way"

#8

The interests, objectives, and grand designs of the
imperialists are not *our* interests—they are not the
interests of the great majority of people in the U.S. nor
of the overwhelming majority of people in the world
as a whole. And the difficulties the imperialists have
gotten themselves into in pursuit of these interests must
be seen, and responded to, not from the point of view
of the imperialists and their interests, but from the point
of view of the great majority of humanity and the basic
and urgent need of humanity for a different and better
world, for another way.

Bringing Forward Another Way, *Revolution* #83, March 25, 2007

#9

Much has been presented by our party on how the world arena is decisive and on the question of how to correctly view the internal and external factors in this era of imperialism—on the relationship between the process of revolution in a particular country and the process of the advance from the bourgeois epoch to the epoch of communism on a world scale and how the contradiction and struggle within particular countries is integrated into that overall process and determined primarily by *its* motion and development.... This doesn't mean of course that you try to make revolution irrespective of the conditions in different parts of the world or the conditions within particular countries, but it means that even in approaching that you proceed from the point of view of the world arena as most decisive and the overall interests of the world proletariat as paramount. And that is not merely a good idea. It has a very material foundation, which has been laid by the system of imperialism.

> *Advancing the World Revolutionary Movement:*
> *Questions of Strategic Orientation*, revcom.us
> (quote originally published 1984)

#10

We can't be simple-minded if we're going to actually do what needs to be done, especially if we are going to make the kind of revolution we need to make. You have to look at what's been building in this society for quite a while now.

It's helpful to look at it kind of like a pyramid....And if you look at this kind of pyramid thing, on the top of this pyramid is the ruling class and its different political representatives, which (even though it may be a bit oversimplified) we can look at as the Democrats on one side and the Republicans on the other. And for decades now these people who are grouped around Bush and the kind of people that they represent have been working and preparing a whole thing in society—a whole infrastructure you might call it—a whole structure within the society itself that could move this society in a whole different way towards a fascistic kind of thing when things come to that.

Look at this whole religious fundamentalist thing they've got. This is an effort to deliberately build up a base of people, millions and millions and millions of people, who are frightened by the idea of thinking— I'm serious—people who cannot deal with all the "complicatedness," all the complexity of modern society, who want simple absolute answers to the complexities of this society....

On the other hand, here are the Democrats at the top of this pyramid (on the so-called "left"). Who are the people that they try to appeal to—not that the Democrats represent their interests, but who are the people that the Democrats try to appeal to at the base, on the other side of this pyramid, so to speak? All the people who stand for progressive kinds of things, all the people who are oppressed in this society. For the Democrats, a big part of their role is to keep all those people confined within the bourgeois, the mainstream, electoral process...and to get them back into it when they have drifted away from—or broken out of—that framework....

This is significant in itself but it also demonstrates a positive potential in terms of revolution. I'm not saying that we are on the threshold of revolution right now, but just looking down the road, and looking at the potential, one of the things that leads to a revolutionary situation is that millions and millions of people feel that something is intolerable. They want certain leaders at the top of society to lead them in doing something about it, but those leaders are not in the position to and don't want to lead them in doing it—so whom do they turn to? The people who are willing and determined to lead them to do it and to take it somewhere. So this is a situation that's full of great danger; but the same situation—or the other side of the contradiction—is that it holds much positive potential for struggle now and for revolution as things unfold.

The Coming Civil War and Repolarization for Revolution in the Present Era, 2005, pp. 1-4

#11

These right-wing politicians (generally grouped within the Republican Party) can, will, and do actively mobilize this essentially fascist social base...yet, on the

other side, the sections of the ruling class that are more
generally represented by the Democratic Party are
very reluctant to, and in fact resistant to, mobilizing...
the base of people whose votes and support in the
bourgeois political arena the Democrats seek to
gain. This (Democratic Party) side of the ruling class
generally is not desirous of—and in fact recoils at the
idea of—calling that base into the streets, mobilizing
them either to take on the opposing forces in the ruling
class and their social base or in general to struggle for
the programs that the Democratic Party itself claims to
represent and actually in some measure does seek to
implement....

As an amplification of the basic point here, it is
important to recognize this: Within the framework of the
capitalist-imperialist system, and with the underlying
dynamics of this system, which fundamentally set the
terms, and the confines, of "official" and "acceptable"
politics, fascism—that is, the imposition of a form of
dictatorship which openly relies on violence and terror
to maintain the rule and the imperatives of the capitalist-
imperialist system—is one possible resolution of the
contradictions that this system is facing—a resolution
that could, at a certain point, more or less correspond to
the compelling needs of this system and its ruling class—
while revolution and real socialism, aiming toward
the final goal of communism, throughout the world, is

also a possible resolution of these contradictions, but one that would most definitely not be acceptable to the capitalist-imperialist ruling class nor compatible with the imperatives of this system!

Unresolved Contradictions, Driving Forces for Revolution – Part I: "Once More on the Coming Civil War... and Repolarization for Revolution," *Revolution* #185, December 13, 2009

#12

If you try to make the Democrats be what they are not and never will be, you will end up being more like what the Democrats actually *are*.

"The Deadly Illusion of the Swinging Pendulum," *Revolution* #20, October 20, 2005

#13

Anybody who thinks for ten seconds about making revolution in a country like the U.S. knows that it is a daunting task, given the whole history of aggression and suppression that the imperialist ruling class has written in the blood of others. And, frankly, most people who have confronted this have given up. I'm not exaggerating. But there is a need not to give up—the masses, throughout the world and, yes, within the U.S. itself, need this. So we must not only *not* give up, we have to break through on this contradiction. And we can't do it without the masses of people. We can't do it until we have a revolutionary situation and a revolutionary people. But when there is such a situation, when masses of people are in motion,

waging determined struggle and demanding a new
and different world, they must not be left to the mercy
of this ruling class, and they must not be left without a
way to win. So that, obviously, is one big challenge.

Reaching for the Heights and Flying Without a Safety Net,
Revolutionary Worker #1210, August 17, 2003

#14

When the whole society is erupting in upheaval and
turmoil, when dramatic changes are taking place and
things are going up for grabs politically, then what was
tolerable, what people have adjusted to—maybe not
just once but several times—becomes intolerable. With
people who are discontented with their situation and
just trying to get through it, when the possibility arises
that they just don't have to do that, then they go through
changes in their thinking and actions very quickly—not
in a straight line toward revolution, but quickly all the
same—and they become more and more open to the
idea of revolution. A lot of people put up with what goes
on all the time in this society and they also know it's
garbage and when they actually see the chance to throw
it away, a lot of them will do so quickly.

Bullets, From the Writings, Speeches & Interviews of Bob Avakian,
Chairman of the Revolutionary Communist Party, USA, 1985
(quote originally published 1980)

#15

In the U.S. you have many different nationalities of
people, and one of the key factors in making a revolution

in this country is going to be developing the struggle,
including among white people, to take on and uproot
the whole history of oppression of Black people, Puerto
Ricans, Chicanos, Native Americans, Asians, and so
on. You are never going to make a revolution in this
country without that being central and pivotal. But
you're also never going to make a revolution without
a vanguard that bases itself on a scientific approach to
these questions—and to every other decisive question—a
vanguard in which everybody contributes and struggles
with each other on the basis of striving to grasp that
scientific approach, and on that basis battles out what is
required to make revolution and to transform society
and the world, to put an end to all oppression.

From *Ike to Mao and Beyond: My Journey from Mainstream America
to Revolutionary Communist, A Memoir by Bob Avakian*, 2005

#16
An Appeal to Those the System Has Cast Off

Here I am speaking not only to prisoners but to those
whose life is lived on the desperate edge, whether or
not they find some work; to those without work or even
homes; to all those the system and its enforcers treat as
so much human waste material.

Raise your sights above the degradation and madness,
the muck and demoralization, above the individual battle
to survive and to "be somebody" on the terms of the
imperialists—of fouler, more monstrous criminals than

mythology has ever invented or jails ever held. Become a part of the human saviors of humanity: the gravediggers of this system and the bearers of the future communist society.

This is not just talk or an attempt to make poetry here: there are great tasks to be fulfilled, great struggles to be carried out, and yes great sacrifices to be made to accomplish all this. But there is a world to save—and to win—and in that process those the system has counted as nothing can count for a great deal. They represent a great reserve force that must become an active force for the proletarian revolution.

Revolution #183, November 15, 2009
(quote originally published 1984)

#17

People say: "You mean to tell me that these youth running around selling drugs and killing each other, and caught up in all kinds of other stuff, can be a backbone of this revolutionary state power in the future?" Yes—but not as they are now, and not without struggle. They weren't always selling drugs and killing each other, and the rest of it—and they don't have to be into all that in the future. Ask yourself: how does it happen that you go from beautiful children to supposedly "irredeemable monsters" in a few years? It's because of the system, and what it does to people—not because of "unchanging and unchangeable human nature."

"There Is No 'Permanent Necessity' for Things To Be This Way"

#18

Even with very real changes in the situation of Black people, as part of the larger changes in the society (and the world) overall—including a growth of the "middle class" among Black people, an increase in college graduates and people in higher paying and prestigious professions, with a few holding powerful positions within the ruling political structures, even to the extent now of a "Black president"—the situation of Black people, and in particular that of millions and millions who are trapped in the oppressive and highly repressive conditions of the inner city ghettos, remains a very acute and profound contradiction for the American imperialist system as a whole and for its ruling class—something which has the potential to erupt totally out of the framework in which they can contain it.

Unresolved Contradictions, Driving Forces for Revolution – Part I, *Revolution* #187, December 27, 2009

#19

There will never be a revolutionary movement in this country that doesn't fully unleash and give expression to the sometimes openly expressed, sometimes expressed in partial ways, sometimes expressed in wrong ways, but deeply, deeply felt desire to be rid of these long centuries of oppression [of Black people]. There's never gonna be a revolution in this country, and there never should be, that doesn't make that one key foundation of what it's all about.

Question and Answer Session of the *7 Talks by Bob Avakian*, 2006, excerpt transcribed in *Revolution* #144, October 5, 2008

#20

There is nothing sacred to us about the USA, as it is presently constituted, or about the borders of the U.S. as they are presently constituted. Quite the opposite.

Revolution #84, April 8, 2007 (quote originally published 1982)

#21

It is hardly conceivable that there could be a revolution in the U.S. which didn't at some point and in various ways significantly interpenetrate with and have mutual interaction and mutual influence with revolutionary struggles being waged by the people in neighboring countries—especially in Central America.

Bullets (quote originally published 1984)

#22

You cannot break all the chains, except one. You cannot say you want to be free of exploitation and oppression, except you want to keep the oppression of women by men. You can't say you want to liberate humanity yet keep one half of the people enslaved to the other half. The oppression of women is completely bound up with the division of society into masters and slaves, exploiters and exploited, and the ending of all such conditions is impossible without the complete liberation of women. All this is why women have a tremendous role to play not only in making revolution but in making sure there is all-the-way revolution. The fury of women can and must be fully unleashed as a mighty force for proletarian revolution.

Revolution #84, April 8, 2007

#23

There is also the importance of the transfer of allegiance—the winning over to revolution and communism—of a section (even today a relatively small section) of the intelligentsia. We have heard, from some people who have been attracted to programs we've done on campuses, that they came to college—often this is younger students—looking for big ideas and were bitterly disappointed at what they have run into, in terms of the prevailing culture and ethos in those universities. This is a significant phenomenon, even if at this point we're only hearing a few people talk about this. The whole swirl of big ideas, intellectual and cultural ferment, and communism contending within that in a lively, compelling way—being, yes, completely outrageous and eminently reasonable— applying the principles I spoke to earlier in terms of, on a scientific foundation, looking to incorporate what can be incorporated, while in some aspects transformed,

from other ideas, conceptions and visions, even from
utopianism: all this is very important in terms of being
able to attract, and win to revolution and communism,
youth among the intelligentsia, as well as people
among the intelligentsia more broadly. Even for a small
section of the intelligentsia to actually be fired up now
about the vision of communism and revolution that
we are bringing forward—that represents something
very significant. We have to persevere to make
breakthroughs in that.

Birds Cannot Give Birth to Crocodiles,
But Humanity Can Soar Beyond the Horizon – Part 2

#24

A genuinely radical, liberating revolt—as opposed
to a reactionary "rebranding" and celebration of
parasitism—must be fostered among the youth in
today's conditions, a revolt within which the need is
powerfully raised for a new society and a new world,
which will move to eliminate the urban/suburban
contradiction, and antagonism, in the context of the
transformation of society, and the world, overall and
the abolition of profound inequalities and divisions—
opposing, overcoming and moving beyond the
parasitism which is such an integral and indispensable
part of the operation and dynamics of imperialism,
and has reached such unprecedented heights in "late
imperial America." In short, we need, in today's

circumstances, a counter-culture that contributes to and is increasingly part of building a movement for revolution—in opposition to a counter-revolutionary culture. We need a culture of radical opposition to the essence of everything that is wrong with this society and system, and the many different manifestations of that; we need an active searching for a radically better world, within which revolution and communism is a powerful and continually growing pole of attraction.

Birds Cannot Give Birth to Crocodiles,
But Humanity Can Soar Beyond the Horizon – Part 2

#25

We also need to be aware of the positive—and in significant ways "subversive of the system"—potential of the assertion of gay "identity" and gay rights, even with the very real contradictions in this, including the narrowing tendencies of "identity politics" as well as conservatizing influences related to traditional marriage, and, for that matter, the campaign to be allowed to be part of the imperialist military while being openly gay. Even with all that, in its principal aspect this has, and can to an even greater degree have, a very positive, "subversive of the system" effect. This is a contradiction which, in the society overall, is "out of the closet." It could be forced back into the closet, and underground, with not only the stronger assertion of the kind of fascist movement that is being supported

and fostered by powerful ruling class forces in this
period, but with the actual assumption of a fascist
form of bourgeois dictatorship. But the struggle against
the oppression of gay people is not going to be easily
suppressed. We should understand the potential of this
as well, and the need to relate correctly to this, to foster
the further development of its positive potential and its
contribution to the movement for revolution.

Birds Cannot Give Birth to Crocodiles,
But Humanity Can Soar Beyond the Horizon – Part 2

#26
You are not going to bring forward a revolutionary
force and a communist movement among the basic
masses, on anything like the scale that is necessary,
and potentially realizable, without there being the
development of political ferment and political resistance
broadly—and, yes, the development of a revolutionary
and communist current—among the middle strata. In
the absence of that, the basic masses are going to say
to you—and they're going to have a point—that "we'll
never get anywhere, we're going to be surrounded,
everybody's going to oppose us, and we're just going
to be viciously crushed once again." On the other hand,
you can't hinge the development of a revolutionary
force and a communist movement among the basic
masses, and in society in general, on developments
among even the progressive section of the middle strata
or among the middle strata more broadly. That's not

mainly where it's going to come out of. So we have to get the dialectics of this correctly.

Bringing Forward Another Way, Revolution #96, July 22, 2007

#27

We are not going to make revolution by trying to superimpose on reality a model of how a socialist transformation is "supposed" to take place....This has to do with the separation of the communist movement from the labor movement, and what are the implications of that in general and specifically in terms of revolution in a country like this....

There is the reality that what we are about does have to be a proletarian revolution, in the sense of its grounding in the most fundamental and largest interests of the proletariat as a class: advancing human society to communism and emancipating all humanity. But this is not a revolution that is going to be made solely by even real proletarians—those in what Lenin referred to as the lower and deeper sections of the working class—and it is certainly not going to be made in some sort of stereotypical "classical" form by "THE WORKING CLASS." In fact, most of the forces who will most actively carry out the fight for the seizure of power—and even those actively involved to a large degree in revolutionary work before the conditions emerge to wage the struggle for the seizure of power—will very likely be mainly <u>not</u> proletarians in the strict sense....

The most bedrock force for revolution will include
"lower and deeper" sections of the proletariat, certainly,
to again use Lenin's phrase. It will include many
immigrants among them. And there is a particular
role which we need to explore further in terms of the
youth among the immigrants. But it will also be, and
perhaps will largely be, basic masses, particularly those
concentrated in the inner cities—many of whom are not
strictly speaking part of the proletarian class—who will
make up this most bedrock force. So this underscores
again why we have to have a living scientific
approach, and a living scientific method, in relation to
transforming reality.

Birds Cannot Give Birth to Crocodiles,
But Humanity Can Soar Beyond the Horizon – Part 2

#28

It is true that we cannot, by our mere will, or even
merely by our actions themselves, transform the
objective conditions in a qualitative sense—into a
revolutionary situation. This cannot be done *merely*
by our operating on, or reacting back on, the objective
conditions through our conscious initiative. On the
other hand....nobody can say exactly what the conscious
initiative of the revolutionaries might be capable of
producing, in reacting upon the objective situation at
any given time—in part because nobody can predict all
the other things that all the different forces in the world
will be doing. Nobody's understanding can encompass
all that at a given time. We can identify trends and

patterns, but there is the role of accident as well as the role of causality. And there is the fact that, although changes in what's objective for us won't come entirely, or perhaps not even mainly, through our "working on" the objective conditions (in some direct, one-to-one sense), nevertheless our "working on" them can bring about certain changes within a given framework of objective conditions *and*—in conjunction with and as part of a "mix," together with many other elements, including other forces acting on the objective situation from their own viewpoints—this can, under certain circumstances, be part of the coming together of factors which *does* result in a qualitative change. And, again, it is important to emphasize that nobody can know exactly how all that will work out.

Revolution is not made by "formulas," or by acting in accordance with stereotypical notions and preconceptions—it is a much more living, rich, and complex process than that. But it is an essential characteristic of revisionism (phony communism which has replaced a revolutionary orientation with a gradualist, and ultimately reformist one) to decide and declare that until some *deus ex machina*—some god-like EXTERNAL FACTOR—intervenes, there can be no essential change in the objective conditions and the most we can do, at any point, is to accept the given framework and work within it, rather than (as we have very correctly formulated it) *constantly straining against the limits* of the objective framework and seeking to *transform the objective conditions to the maximum degree possible* at any given time, always being tense to the possibility of different things coming together which bring about (or make possible the bringing about of) an actual qualitative rupture and leap in the objective situation....

So, if you are looking at things only in a linear way, then you only see the possibilities that are straight ahead—you have a kind of blinders on. On the other hand, if you have a correct, dialectical materialist approach, you recognize that many things can happen that are unanticipated, and you have to be constantly tense to that possibility while consistently working to transform necessity into freedom. So, again, that is a basic point of orientation.

Making Revolution and Emancipating Humanity – Part 2,
Revolution #113, December 23, 2007

#29

What has been said so far, concerning "solid core with a lot of elasticity," relates very closely to the next point I want to get into, which is *the "parachute" point*: **the concentration of things at the time of the seizure of power, and then the "opening out" again after the consolidation of power.**

This is a general principle as to how revolution goes, and it also has more specific application to a country like this, and this country in particular. Whatever the path to power in a particular country…at the time when countrywide political power can be seized, things become "compressed" politically. A lot of the diverse political trends and currents that are in opposition to the established power either become politically paralyzed and/or they become compressed in and around the one core that actually embodies the means for breaking through what needs to be broken through to meet the immediately, urgently felt needs of broad masses of people who are demanding radical change. This happens specifically and in a concentrated way when that need to break through to actually seize power is not just some sort of long-term strategic objective and consideration, but becomes immediately posed; when, along with that and as part of that, other programs which are seeking social change become paralyzed in the attempts to implement them—run up against their limitations which, on a mass scale, causes people to reject them and to rally from them to the one program that actually does represent the way to break through.

Things tend to become compressed at that point, as when a parachute closes up. And one of the things that has not been sufficiently understood—and has led to mistakes, in its not being correctly understood and dealt with—is the fact that, while this is a very real and important and necessary ingredient, in an overall sense, of actually being able to have the alignment that makes it possible to go for revolution, this is something that comes into being at the concentration point of a

revolutionary situation but *not* something that will
continue in the same way after that point has been
passed, regardless of how that situation is resolved—
not only if the revolutionary attempt fails or is defeated,
*but even if it is successful and results in the establishment of
a new, radically different state power*. Even then, after that
situation has passed, and as things go forward in the
new society, the "parachute" will "open back up" and
"spread out."...

So here is where, after power is consolidated, "the
parachute opens back out." In other words, all the
diversity of political programs, outlooks, inclinations,
and so on...all these things assert, or reassert,
themselves. And if you go on the assumption that,
because people all rallied to you at that particular
moment when only your program could break
through—if you identify that with the notion that
they're all going to be marching in lockstep with you
and in agreement with you at every point all the way
to communism—you are going to make very serious
errors. This is a very important point in general
in terms of revolution and, obviously, would have
particular and important application in a country like
the U.S. And, obviously, this relates to **solid core with a
lot of elasticity**.

"The Basis, the Goals, and the Methods of the
Communist Revolution," *Revolution* #47, May 21, 2006

#30

Some Principles for Building a Movement for Revolution

At every point, we must be searching out the key concentrations of social contradictions and the methods and forms which can strengthen the political consciousness of the masses, as well as their fighting capacity and organization in carrying out political resistance against the crimes of this system; which can increasingly bring the necessity, and the possibility, of a radically different world to life for growing numbers of people; and which can strengthen the understanding and determination of the advanced, revolutionary-minded masses in particular to take up our strategic objectives not merely as far-off and essentially abstract goals (or ideals) but as things to be actively striven for and built toward.

The objective and orientation must be to carry out work which, together with the development of the objective situation, can transform the political terrain, so that the legitimacy of the established order, and the right and ability of the ruling class to rule, is called into question, in an acute and active sense, throughout society; so that resistance to this system becomes increasingly broad, deep and determined; so that the "pole" and the organized vanguard force of revolutionary communism is greatly strengthened; and so that, at the decisive time, this advanced force is able to lead the struggle of millions, and tens of millions, to make revolution.

Revolution #202, May 30, 2010

#31

We hear from masses of people—and I've seen this in reports recently—statements or sentiments along the following lines: "I know revolution is needed," or "I know revolution is what's gotta happen at some point," but "what do we do now, what do we do in the meantime?"

Answer? Make revolution. Fight the Power, and Transform the People, for Revolution. Prepare minds and organize forces for the time when a revolutionary situation and a revolutionary people, in the millions and millions, emerges. Work actively and consciously to bring this time closer and to bring things to where we are in the best position to act decisively when this does come about. Devote your life, energy, daring and creativity to confronting, fighting through and overcoming the obstacles to making this happen, and to winning more and more people to doing the same.

> *Ruminations and Wranglings: On the Importance of*
> *Marxist Materialism, Communism as a Science,*
> *Meaningful Revolutionary Work, and a Life with Meaning,*
> *Revolution #175, September 6, 2009*

#32

What is involved in "Enriched What Is To Be Done-ism" is sharply and scientifically exposing the system, bringing to light the causes and reasons for the oppression that different sections of the people suffer and the outrages that masses of people detest; showing, in a living way, how all this is rooted in and has as its source the system of capitalism-imperialism, which

perpetuates and enforces this on a daily basis and in
horrific dimensions; illustrating, through the application
of a scientific, dialectical materialist method, how different
sections of the people tend to respond to different
events in society and the world, and how this relates to
their position within the overall production and social
relations; bringing forward and setting before all, and
boldly struggling for, our revolutionary and communist
orientation and convictions; and mobilizing people, yes,
to fight back against oppression but to do so on the basis
and with the orientation and aim of building a movement
for revolution, toward the goal of sweeping aside the
capitalist-imperialist system, bringing into being a new,
socialist system and continuing to advance, together with
people struggling throughout the world, toward the final
goal of communism; and setting before the masses of
people not only the goals of the revolution and the basic
strategy for making revolution, as embodied in the line
and policies of the party, but also the problems of making
revolution, involving growing numbers of the masses in
grappling with and helping to resolve these contradictions
in the direction of revolution and communism.

Unresolved Contradictions, Driving Forces for Revolution – Part I,
Revolution #188, January 10, 2010

#33

Addressing all this, through applying the basic
orientation and approach that Lenin argues for in
What Is To Be Done?—and as this is further "enriched"
in the ways I have referred to here—is the role of the

communist newspaper in building the revolutionary movement. Our Party's newspaper, *Revolution*, has to continue to sharpen its ability to play this role, at the same time as comrades in the Party—and growing numbers of people who, at any given time, are not yet in the Party, but are, in a basic sense, partisan to or supportive of the Party's aims and actions—have to wield the newspaper with this kind of orientation.... This is (to invoke again Lenin's phrasing) "the better part of preparation"—even though it is, in a sense, indirect preparation—for the future struggle for power....Wielding the newspaper in this way is, in the conditions that obtain in countries like the U.S., the most important means of hastening while awaiting.

Making Revolution and Emancipating Humanity – Part 2,
Revolution #113, December 23, 2007

#34

If you want to know about, and work toward, a different world—and if you want to stand up and fight back against what's being done to people—this is where you go. You go to this Party, you take up this Party's newspaper, you get into this Party's leader and what he's bringing forward.

Making Revolution and Emancipating Humanity – Part 2,
Revolution #116, January 20, 2008

#35

When we're taking this out, and working to build this culture of appreciation, promotion, and popularization [in relation to the leadership of Bob Avakian], we are not doing so in order to build a cult around a person, in some religious sense. We're doing so in order to enable people to engage the most advanced understanding we have of where society and humanity needs to go, and can go, what this body of work and method and approach has to do with *that* and why it's important *in relation to that*— why, in reality, it is indispensable for masses of people to engage with this in relation to—to serve, and to advance towards—*that*, and not anything else. Even the aspect, which is secondary but not unimportant—the aspect of the person Bob Avakian—is important *only* in the framework of, and on the basis of, being a revolutionary communist leader, the leader of a communist vanguard party which is capable of leading people toward the goal of revolution and ultimately communism—which has to continue developing its ability to do this, but has a basic foundation for actually leading people toward that goal. That is the point of all this.

Making Revolution and Emancipating Humanity – Part 2,
Revolution #115, January 13, 2008

#36
The notion of "unchanging human nature" is completely erroneous, and the idea that people are naturally selfish is nothing but another tautology. As Marx and Engels pointed out in the Communist Manifesto, this amounts to nothing other than saying that, with the domination of the bourgeois mode of production, the dominant thinking and ways of acting will be in accordance with the dictates of the bourgeois

mode of production. As the Manifesto also puts it, the ruling ideas of any age are ever the ideas of the ruling class—and these ideas are spread and have great influence not only within the ruling class itself but also among other sections of the population, including the class (or classes) most brutally exploited and oppressed by the ruling class. But, as spoken to earlier, from era to era in human history, and even within the confines of the era of capitalist rule, when there are upsurges of mass struggle people undergo great changes in their ways of thinking and of relating to each other. In a basic sense, this is, and can only be, temporary and partial, as long as there is not a successful revolution and a radical qualitative change in society as a whole. Nonetheless, especially in circumstances of great social upheaval and struggle against the established order, people go through great changes in their thinking and their way of relating to each other. If this were not so, revolutions could never be made and social relations could never be changed by people consciously reacting back upon them. Yet, looking at the history of human beings and their society, this has happened frequently—radical changes in society as a whole have been brought about repeatedly—and this will happen again, in a far greater and more radical way, with the communist revolution.

Away With All Gods! Unchaining the Mind
and Radically Changing the World, 2008

Supplement

The following is an important statement which was written on the basis of drawing from key strategic principles set forth in the publications of the Revolutionary Communist Party—and in particular the works of Bob Avakian. For these reasons, this statement is included here. It was published in *Revolution* #226, March 6, 2011, and is posted at revcom.us.

A Statement from the Revolutionary Communist Party

On the Strategy for Revolution

Under this system of capitalism, so many in this society and so much of humanity are forced to endure great hardship and suffering, exploitation, injustice and brutality, while wars and the ongoing destruction of the natural environment threaten the very future of humanity. In the *Constitution for the New Socialist Republic in North America (Draft Proposal)* our Party has set forth an inspiring vision, and concrete measures, for the building of a new society, a socialist society, aiming for the final goal of a communist world, where human beings everywhere would be free of relations of exploitation and oppression and destructive antagonistic conflicts, and could be fit caretakers of the earth. But to make this a reality, we need revolution.

Many people insist, "there could never be a revolution in this country: the powers-that-be are too powerful, the people are too messed up and too caught up in going along with the way things are, the revolutionary forces are too small." This is wrong—revolution is possible.

Of course revolution cannot happen with conditions and people the way they are now. But revolution can come about as conditions and people are moved to change, because of developments in the world and because of the work of revolutionaries...as people come to see that **things do not have to be this way**...as they come to understand why things are the way they are and how things could be radically different...and as they are inspired and organized to join the revolutionary movement and build up its forces.

Revolution will not be made by acting all crazy—trying to bring down this powerful system when there is not yet a basis for that—or by just waiting for "one fine day" when revolution will somehow magically become possible. Revolution requires consistent work building for revolution, based on a serious, scientific understanding of what it takes to actually get to the point of revolution, and how to have a real chance of winning.

In order for revolution to be real there must be: **a**

revolutionary crisis, and a revolutionary people, num-
bering in the millions and led by a far-seeing, highly
organized and disciplined revolutionary party. Clearly,
this is not the reality now. So, how can this come about?
And what is the strategic plan?

The potential for a revolutionary crisis lies within
the very nature of this capitalist system itself—with its
repeated economic convulsions, its unemployment and
poverty, its profound inequalities, its discrimination and
degradation, its brutality, torture and wars, its wanton
destruction. All this causes great suffering. And at times
it leads to crisis on one level or another—sudden jolts
and breakdowns in the "normal functioning" of society,
which compel many people to question and to resist
what they usually accept. No one can say in advance
exactly what will happen in these situations—how deep
the crisis may go, in what ways and to what extent it
might pose challenges to the system as a whole, and to
what degree and in what ways it might call forth unrest
and rebellion among people who are normally caught
up in, or feel powerless to stand up against, what this
system does. But two points are very important:

1) Such "jolts" in the "normal functioning" of things,
even if they do not develop all the way to a fundamental
crisis for the system as a whole, do create situations in
which many more people are searching for answers and
open to considering radical change. The work of building

the movement for revolution must be consistently carried out at all times, but in these situations of sharp breaks with the "normal routine" there is greater possibility, and greater potential, to make advances. This must be fully recognized and built on to the greatest degree possible, so that <u>through such situations, leaps are made in building up the movement and the organized forces for revolution, creating in this way a stronger basis from which to work for further advances.</u>

2) In certain situations, <u>major events</u> or <u>big changes</u> can happen in society and the world and <u>can come together</u> in such a way that <u>the system is shaken to its foundations</u>...<u>deep cracks</u> appear and magnify <u>within the ruling structures and institutions</u>...the <u>raw relations of oppression</u> are more <u>sharply exposed</u>...<u>conflicts among the powers-that-be</u> deepen, and cannot be easily resolved, and it becomes <u>much more difficult for them to hold things together</u> under their control <u>and keep people down</u>. In this kind of situation, for great numbers of people, <u>the "legitimacy" of the current system, and the right and ability of the ruling powers to keep on ruling, can be called seriously and directly into question</u>, with millions hungering for <u>a radical change that only a revolution can bring about</u>.

More needs to be learned, and will be learned, about how the revolutionary struggle can win when these conditions have been brought into being, but <u>the basic</u>

<u>strategic conception and approach has been developed</u> for actually <u>defeating and dismantling</u> the oppressive forces and institutions of <u>this system</u>—and bringing into being new institutions of a new, revolutionary system—<u>when there is a revolutionary crisis and a revolutionary people</u>. (This basic conception and approach is set forth in "On the Possibility of Revolution"—and this is also included in the pamphlet *Revolution and Communism: A Foundation and Strategic Orientation*—published by our Party.)

But the possibility of revolution will never really ripen unless <u>those who recognize the need for revolution are preparing the ground for this politically and ideologically even now</u>: working to influence the thinking of people in a revolutionary direction, organizing them into the struggle against this system, and winning growing numbers to become actively involved in building the movement for revolution. This is what our Party is all about, and what we mean when we say we are **"hastening** while awaiting" the changes that make revolution possible. This is <u>the key to breaking through</u> the situation where there are not yet the necessary conditions and forces to make revolution, but those conditions and forces will <u>never</u> be brought into being by <u>just waiting</u> for them to appear.

All along the way, both in more "normal times" and especially in times of sharp breaks with the "normal routine," it is necessary to be <u>working consistently</u> to accumulate forces—to prepare minds and organize people in growing numbers—for revolution, among all those who can be rallied to the revolutionary cause. Among the millions and millions who catch hell in the hardest ways every day under this system. But also among many others who may not, on a daily basis, feel the hardest edge of this system's oppression but are demeaned and degraded, are alienated and often outraged, by what this system does, the relations among people it promotes and enforces, the brutality this embodies.

What is the way to carry out this work? **Fight the Power, and Transform the People, for Revolution.** This is a big part of the answer. People need to fight back, and people do fight back, against the many ways human beings, and the environment, are exploited, degraded, ravaged and even destroyed by this system. But to make that fight more powerful—and, more, to carry it through to put an end to all this—people need to learn that the fundamental problem is this capitalist system, and the solution is getting rid of this system and bringing into being a new system, socialism, aiming for the final goal of a communist world. **Fight the Power, and Transform the People, for Revolution** is a key part of our strategic approach, which provides a way for the Party to unite with and give leadership to people to change themselves as they take part in the struggle to change the world...to lift their heads and broaden their vision, to recognize what kind of world is possible, what their real interests are, and who their real friends and real enemies are, as they rise up against this system...to take up a revolutionary viewpoint and revolutionary values and morals as they join with others to resist this system's crimes and build up the basis for the ultimate all-out revolutionary struggle to sweep this system away and bring in a whole new way of organizing society, a whole new way of being...to become emancipators of humanity.

For all this to happen, and for the revolution to have a real chance of winning, leadership is essential. And there is such leadership. But there is also much work to do.

To support and strengthen our Party as the overall leadership of this revolution. The more our Party's revolutionary viewpoint and strategy is spread and gains influence throughout society...the more that people come to understand and agree with what the Party is all about, and join its ranks on that basis...the more the Party's "reach" extends to every corner of the country... the greater its organizational strength and its ability to withstand and to lead people forward in the face of government repression aimed at crushing resistance and killing off revolution—the more the basis for revolution will be prepared and the more favorable the chance of winning.

To learn from the Chairman of our Party, Bob Avakian, spread the knowledge and influence of his pathbreaking leadership, and defend and protect this rare and precious leader. Bob Avakian has dedicated his life since the 1960s to the cause of revolution and communism. While providing practical leadership to the Party and the revolutionary movement, he has deeply studied and summed up the world historical experience of the communist revolution and the socialist societies it has brought into being—the great achievements and the serious problems and errors—and has studied many other fields of human experience and knowledge. He has advanced the science of communism and made decisive breakthroughs in the theory, method, and strategy of revolution and the final goal of communism throughout the world. It is crucial for growing numbers of people to know about and study his talks and writings...to defend and protect him...to take up the leadership he is providing, which opens new pathways for revolution.

To much more fully wield our Party's newspaper, *Revolution.* This plays a pivotal role in carrying out our strategy. Through publishing works of Bob Avakian, and through many different articles, interviews, letters, graphics, and other features, *Revolution* enables people to really understand and act to radically change the world.... It gives people a living picture and scientific analysis of what is going on in the world, and why....It exposes the true nature of this system, and shows how major events in society and the world are concentrations of the basic contradictions of this oppressive and putrid system....It brings alive the need and possibility for revolution and a whole new society and world....It heightens the ability of growing numbers of people, in all parts of this country, to act politically in a unified way, and to wrestle with and help find solutions to the problems of our movement, on the basis of a growing revolutionary consciousness....It is the key instrument in developing an organized political network, among the most oppressed and other sections of the people, which can have a growing impact on the political scene and the society (and the world) as a whole, building up the forces of revolution and influencing ever broader numbers of people....It provides a foundation and a means for extending the "reach" of the revolutionary movement and building up bases for this movement—in neighborhoods, where people work and go to school, and wherever people come together—and especially where they resist and rebel against this system.

All this can enable the revolutionary movement, with the Party at the core, to confront and overcome the very real obstacles in its path...to advance and grow, through ongoing work, and through a series of critical leaps in times of sudden breaks and ruptures with the "normal routine"...to prepare the ground, and accumulate forces, for revolution—and have a real chance at winning. It is how <u>thousands can be brought forward and oriented,</u> <u>organized and trained in a revolutionary way</u>, while beginning to reach and influence millions more, even before there is a revolutionary situation...and then, <u>when</u> <u>there is a revolutionary situation, those thousands can</u> <u>be a backbone and pivotal force in winning millions</u> to revolution and organizing them in the struggle <u>to carry</u> <u>the revolution through</u>.

For those who have hungered for, who have dreamed of, a whole different world, without the madness and torment of what this system brings every day...those who have dared to hope that such a world could be possible... and even those who, up to now, would like to see this, but have accepted that this could never happen...there is a place and a role, a need and a means, for thousands now and ultimately millions to contribute to building this movement for revolution, in many different ways, big and small—with ideas and with practical involvement, with support, and with questions and criticisms. Get together with our Party, learn more about this movement and become a part of it as you learn, acting in unity with others in this country, and throughout the world, aiming for the very challenging but tremendously inspiring and liberating—and, yes, possible—goal of emancipating all of humanity through revolution and advancing to a communist world, free of exploitation and oppression.

CHAPTER 4
UNDERSTANDING THE WORLD

#1

Oppressed people who are unable or unwilling to confront reality as it actually is, are condemned to remain enslaved and oppressed.

*Away With All Gods! Unchaining the Mind
and Radically Changing the World*, 2008

#2

Why have I, in my writings and talks, repeatedly emphasized that communism represents the most consistently, thoroughly, systematically, and comprehensively scientific outlook and method? Well, to introduce a formulation and refrain that you'll hear repeatedly through this talk, the main reason I do it is because it is <u>true</u>! And it is important.

"Views on Socialism and Communism: A Radically New Kind of
State, A Radically Different and Far Greater Vision of Freedom,"
Revolution #39, March 19, 2006

#3

There is a glaring lack of understanding—and a crying need for people to understand—that there is a system whose basic contradictions and dynamics set the terms of things in a fundamental sense; and for people to be given, in a living and compelling way, a materialist analysis and a materialist estimate, as Lenin put it, of how this system actually works and the role of different classes and social forces in relation to all this.

Ruminations and Wranglings: On the Importance of Marxist Materialism, Communism as a Science, Meaningful Revolutionary Work, and a Life with Meaning, Revolution #169, June 28, 2009

#4

Communism, as a world outlook and method, is both thoroughly and consistently materialist and thoroughly and consistently dialectical, and that is true of no other world outlook and method. Communism reflects, in its outlook and method, the fundamental truth that <u>all of reality consists of matter in motion</u> and nothing else: It grasps each of these aspects—that all reality consists of <u>matter and nothing else</u>; and that, as Engels put it, <u>the mode of existence of matter is motion</u>, that all of matter is constantly moving and changing, and that this leads to qualitative leaps and ruptures—and communism grasps the dialectical relation between these things.

"Views on Socialism and Communism," *Revolution #39, March 19, 2006*

#5

Everything that is actually true is good for the proletariat, all truths can help us get to communism.

"Bob Avakian in a Discussion with Comrades on Epistemology: On Knowing and Changing the World," *Observations on Art and Culture, Science and Philosophy, 2005*

#6

Knowing about actual reality—and continually learning more about it—is vitally important for humanity and its future; it is vitally important not only for people in the sciences and the academic world but for the brutally oppressed and exploited people of the earth, who must and can be the backbone and driving force of a revolution to throw off and put an end to all forms of exploitation and oppression, throughout the globe—to be the emancipators not only of themselves but ultimately of all humanity. Confronting reality as it actually is—and as it is changing and developing—and understanding the underlying and driving forces in this, is crucial in order to play a decisive and leading role in bringing about this revolution and ushering in a whole new era in human history, which will shatter and remove forever not only the material chains—the economic, social and political shackles of exploitation and oppression—that enslave people in today's world but also the mental chains, the ways of thinking and the culture, that correspond to and reinforce those material chains. In the Communist Manifesto, Karl Marx and Frederick Engels, who founded the communist movement over 150 years ago, declared that the communist revolution, and its emancipating principles, methods, and aims, involves a "radical rupture" not only with the traditional property relations that enslave people, in one form or another,

but also a radical rupture with all traditional ideas that
reflect and reinforce those traditional property relations.

"'A Leap of Faith' and a Leap to Rational Knowledge:
Two Very Different Kinds of Leaps, Two Radically Different
Worldviews and Methods," *Revolution* #10, July 31, 2005

#7

We have to rupture more fully with instrumentalism—
with notions of making reality an "instrument" of
our objectives, of distorting reality to try to make
it serve our ends, of "political truth." The dynamic
of "truths that make us cringe" is part of what can
be driving us forward. This can help call forth that
ferment so that we can understand reality. This is
scientific materialist objectivity. If you go deeply
enough and understand that these contradictions
now posed could lead to a different era based on the
resolution of those contradictions, then you want to
set in motion a dynamic where people *are* bringing
out your shortcomings. Not that every mistake should
be brought out in a way to overwhelm everything
we're trying to do, but in a strategic sense [we should]
welcome this and not try to manage it too much—you
want that, the back and forth.

"Bob Avakian in a Discussion with Comrades
on Epistemology: On Knowing and Changing the World"

#8

Many different new things, positive and negative, are
going to be brought into being not only by us but by
other people, and it's a question of how do we view

and relate to them, how do we unite with them but
also struggle with them, how do we sift through and
help others sift through and synthesize what's correct
and progressive and even revolutionary within them
and cast off those things that are the opposite, that are
backward or are incorrect.

"We Can't Know Everything – So We Should Be Good
at Learning," *Observations on Art and Culture, Science and
Philosophy*, 2005 (quote originally published 2002)

#9

The people who run this country wouldn't recognize
the truth if they had a head-on collision with it.

*Bullets, From the Writings, Speeches & Interviews of Bob Avakian,
Chairman of the Revolutionary Communist Party, USA*, 1985

#10

For humanity to <u>advance beyond</u> a state in which
"might makes right"—and where things ultimately
come down to raw power relations—will require, as
a fundamental element in this advance, an approach
to understanding things (an epistemology) which
recognizes that reality and truth are <u>objective</u> and do
not vary in accordance with, nor depend on, different
"narratives" and how much "authority" an idea (or
"narrative") may have behind it, or how much power
and force can be wielded on behalf of any particular
idea or "narrative," at any given point.

"Some Observations on the Culture Wars: Textbooks, Movies,
Sham Shakespearean Tragedies and Crude Lies,"
Revolution #198, April 11, 2010

#11

What people think is <u>part of</u> objective reality, but
objective reality is not <u>determined</u> by what people think.

Revolution #196, March 28, 2010

#12

The battle around evolution is important in its own
right, *and* it has a great deal to do with the battle for
revolution. It is, first of all, a battle in the realm of
epistemology—over questions of what is truth and
whether and how human beings can acquire a true
understanding of reality. Are we going to proceed
according to a scientific approach—investigating reality,
to accumulate experience and evidence about reality, and
then drawing rational conclusions? Or, are we going to
blindly adopt an outmoded way of understanding how
the world works and what its driving forces are, and
insist upon *superimposing that on reality* and on smashing
down anything which conflicts with that non-rational (or
irrational) approach? Are we going to insist on *a priori*
notions of truth—dogmatic assumptions which are not
drawn from reality and not testable in reality—and rule
out of order things which *are* drawn from reality and
have been tested and shown in reality to be true?

Away With All Gods!

#13

There is not one human nature. There is not some
uniform and unchanging way that everybody is and

how everybody sees the world. Human nature has different meanings in different times and for different classes and groups in society.

> *Revolution: Why It's Necessary, Why It's Possible, What It's All About, a film of a talk by Bob Avakian.* Available at revolutiontalk.net and in a DVD set from RCP Publications.

#14

Our party calls on people and says the first thing you should do is to raise your head up and ask, "why." Ask "why" whenever they tell you to do anything, and for that matter, ask why whenever *we* say you should do anything. Because we're not afraid of people questioning us. We're not afraid of people digging into what we have to say. We're not afraid of people criticizing us and struggling with us, because we stand on the basis of the revolutionary science that represents the interests of the masses of people. And if our grasp of that science is not complete, if our grasp of that science is wrong in this or that particular aspect, or if the way in which we're applying it doesn't correspond fully to the interests of the masses of people, then we're not afraid—in fact, we insist—that people come forward and call us out and question us and struggle with us and criticize us. That's the only way that we're ever going to be able to bring that revolutionary science to the masses of people, and for them to take it up and wield it as a weapon to win their own emancipation.

> *Bullets* (quote originally published 1980)

#15

The truth will not set us free, in and of itself, but we will not get free without the truth.

Away With All Gods!

#16

What is the role of religion—and is it really harmful? A lot of people say: "Alright, maybe it's not true, but what harm does it do? It makes people feel better—a loved one dies and they want to believe that the loved one went to heaven, and when they die they'll be reunited with that loved one. Or something terrible happens in someone's life, and she wants to take comfort and solace in the belief that there is some larger purpose, directed by some god, that makes this have meaning in some form. How can that do any harm?"

Well, let's paraphrase Stevie Wonder's song "Superstition": "When you believe in things and they don't exist and you suffer, superstition's in your way." (Actually he says, "When you believe in things that you don't understand..."—but it's the same point.) You do suffer when you believe in things that you not only don't understand, but that, by definition, you *can't* understand. And whether or not Stevie Wonder had religion in mind in saying this, it definitely applies to religion.

Away With All Gods!

#17

The notion of a god, or gods, was created by humanity, in its infancy, out of ignorance. This has been perpetuated by ruling classes, for thousands of years since then, to serve their interests in exploiting and dominating the majority of people and keeping them enslaved to ignorance and irrationality.

Bringing about a new, and far better, world and future for humanity means overthrowing such exploiting classes and breaking free of and leaving behind forever such enslaving ignorance and irrationality.

Away With All Gods!

#18

Let's call this what it is—it is a *slave mentality*, with which people are being indoctrinated. All this "thank you Jesus!" is a slave mentality.

Away With All Gods!

#19

As for my friends, today there's all this nonsense about how Black people are just inherently religious—and that's a whole thing that gets me pissed off, it's just bullshit. These are socially conditioned things. A lot of my Black friends and a lot of people who influenced me later in life, like the Panthers, were going through the same thing I'd gone through, and recognized that these religious ideas and institutions are human inventions—and not very good ones. So some of my friends were still religious, but many of them were going through the same general kind of emancipating experience that I was in casting off religion.

From Ike to Mao and Beyond: My Journey from Mainstream America to Revolutionary Communist, A Memoir by Bob Avakian, 2005

#20

Every religion in the world believes that every other religion is superstition. And they're all correct.

Revolution #84, April 8, 2007 (quote originally published 1978)

#21

This is an analogy that I have found helpful: Reality is like a fire, like a burning object, and if you want to pick up that burning object and move it, you have to have an instrument with which to do it. If you try to do it bare-handed, the result is not going to be good. That's another way of getting at the role of theory in relation to the larger world that needs to be transformed, in relation to practice, and in particular revolutionary practice, to change the world.

Bringing Forward Another Way, Revolution #93, June 24, 2007

#22

Theory and (political and ideological) line are abstractions from reality which, the more correct they are, the more they can guide us in changing the world in accordance with its actual nature and its actual motion. If you are going to wield theory and line as an instrument to change the world, you have to take it up and wrangle with it in its own right—abstracted from the reality out of which it comes, of which it is a concentration—and to which, yes, as Marx emphasized and we must emphasize, it must be returned in order to change the world. But if you leave out the step of grappling, on the level of abstraction, with theory, you are bound to go astray and land in a pit.

And everybody can deal in abstractions, by the way. It's not only a handful of people who can do this. Revolutionary theory, communist theory, has to be made accessible to masses of people, but they actually engage in abstraction all the time, with different world outlooks. I've never met any basic person, or any person from any stratum, who doesn't have all kinds of theories about all kinds of things—most of them drawn from the bourgeoisie and ultimately reflecting its outlook—although some of them do this only indirectly and appear to be, and to some degree are, ideas and theories that people have "cooked up" on their own, more or less unconsciously reflecting the dominant bourgeois outlook in society. Of course, to make theoretical abstractions that most correctly, deeply and fully reflect reality, in its motion and development, requires taking up the communist world outlook and methodology and increasingly learning to apply this consistently and systematically. And, as Lenin emphasized (in *What Is To Be Done?* and elsewhere), this communist outlook and methodology will not just "come to" the masses of people on their own and spontaneously, but must be brought to them from outside the realm of their direct and immediate experience. But the fact remains that everyone engages in theoretical abstraction of one kind or another— everybody is capable of this—and, fundamentally, it is a question of how are you doing this, with what world outlook and methodology?

Bringing Forward Another Way, Revolution #93, June 24, 2007

#23

During that time and on the way back after the game I was sitting with some Black friends of mine on the football team, and we got into this whole deep conversation about why is there so much racism in this country, why is there so much prejudice and where does it come from, and can it ever change, and how could it change? This was mainly them talking and me listening. And I remember that very, very deeply—I learned a lot more in that one hour than I learned in hours of classroom time, even from some of the better teachers.

From Ike to Mao and Beyond, Chapter 4, "High School"

#24

In terms of science, the scientific method, and in
particular the scientific outlook and method of
communism, it is crucial to constantly be striving
to maintain a spirit and method of critical thinking
and openness to what is new and what challenges
accepted or received wisdom. This involves repeatedly
re-examining what is believed by oneself and/or
the prevailing opinions in society, etc., to be true:
repeatedly subjecting this to further testing and
interrogation from the challenges of those who oppose
this and of reality itself, including the ways that the
ongoing development of material reality may bring to
light new facts—that is, newly discovered or newly
understood aspects of reality which pose challenges to
the accepted wisdom. However, it is very important to
emphasize, this does <u>not</u> mean falling into agnosticism
and relativism, denying objective truth and in particular
acting as if everything must be called into question,
as if nothing is known or can be counted on as being
true, whenever new discoveries, or new theories or
hypotheses, call into question certain ideas previously
determined or thought to be true. The scientific process
and scientific knowledge, and knowledge in general, is
not advanced in this way and cannot be advanced in
this way—at least not in any kind of sustained sense—
but is advanced by proceeding on the basis of what has

previously been established to be true, especially where
this has been established through mutually reinforcing
evidence and rational conclusions drawn from a
range of sources; and then to further probe and learn
about reality and use the accumulated store of human
knowledge, including with regard to methodology, in
evaluating new evidence, new theories, new challenges
to what has been held to be true, and so on.

Ruminations and Wranglings, Revolution #174, August 30, 2009

#25

One time someone wrote me a letter and asked: how
do you read things, do you do what's called "proof-
texting"?—which is a way of reading to refute something.
Do you read it in order to make your point? What he was
referring to was the approach of only looking for things
that confirm what you already believe; for example, you
start out with a disagreement with somebody and in
reading what they write you look for those things that
you don't agree with, things that prove your point, and
then sort of tautologically you go around in a circle. You
end up with: "Aha, it's wrong." And I replied, no I don't
approach things that way. Even things I vehemently
disagree with, going in, I still try to look to see what there
is that they are grappling with, what ideas they may hit
on even inadvertently or may stumble on, or may actually
wrangle with more systematically. There are things to be
learned even from reactionaries. There are things to learn
from reactionaries, even about politics and ideology, let

alone other spheres. That doesn't mean we take up their
outlook or their politics. But there are things to be learned.
And this is an important point of orientation.

*Dictatorship and Democracy, and the Socialist Transition to
Communism, Revolutionary Worker #1250, August 22, 2004*

#26

I have always taken the approach of reading very
broadly. In studying the history of the international
communist movement, I read summations not only
from people who were within that tradition, but also
people from a number of very different viewpoints.
And I've learned more and more the importance of
doing that. Again, I've taken up a principle that Mao
brought forward: Marxism, as he put it, embraces
but does not replace the arts and sciences and all the
different fields of human endeavor. It is necessary to
learn from many different people with many diverse
viewpoints in all these different fields.

From Ike to Mao and Beyond

#27

It is not easy to learn very broadly without losing your
bearings; and it is not easy to hold on to the correct
basic approach and method without getting dogmatic
and mechanical about it and failing to learn everything
you can from many different people with many diverse
viewpoints and experiences. This is a real challenge,

which requires the correct orientation, and hard
work—in contrast to dogmatism, which, as Mao also
emphasized, is the province of "lazy bones."

From Ike to Mao and Beyond

#28

At the same time, while I remain firmly convinced that
the fundamental principles of dialectical materialism,
as I have touched on them here—including that all
reality consists of matter in motion, and that all levels
and forms of matter involve internal contradiction—
are valid and have not been refuted, or called into
question, by what has been learned in physics, or other
fields, it also remains true, without lapsing into an
agnostic orientation—as if we cannot draw definite
conclusions about, and proceed on the basis of, these
fundamental principles—we could all benefit, and
must continue to learn, from further exploration and
grappling with questions concerning the basic character
of reality (matter in motion). This, if approached with a
consistently scientific outlook and method, will serve to
strengthen our ability to grasp, apply and further enrich
dialectical materialism.

"'Crises in Physics,' Crises in Philosophy and Politics,"
Revolution #161, April 12, 2009. Also in *Demarcations: A Journal of
Communist Theory and Polemic*, Issue Number 1, Summer-Fall 2009

#29

So there is a great diversity and richness to human
society as a result not just of the fact that there are
billions of different individuals, but as a result of
this contradiction between the fact that people exist
as individuals while at the same time their lives are
shaped essentially by social and most fundamentally
production relations. This, if you want to put it that
way, is another expression of the "multi-layered and
multi-colored map" metaphor—of understanding the
rich texture and diversity and complexity of reality
and seeing these things as fluid, and (to paraphrase the
Communist Manifesto) not as fixed, fast, and frozen.

Ruminations and Wranglings, Revolution #163, May 1, 2009

#30

People look at what religion calls "the heavens."
They look at the stars, the galaxies. They can see a
small part of the vastness of the universe, and they
can imagine the greater vastness of the universe. Or
they can look on a small scale, look with a microscope
and see a small microbe or whatever, and be amazed
by what goes on internally within that. They can
ponder the relation between what you can see with
a microscope and what you can see with a telescope.
This is an essential quality of human beings. Human
beings will always strive for this. Far from trying to

suppress this, or failing to recognize it, we can and should and will give much fuller expression to it.

Communism will not put an end to—nor somehow involve the suppression of—awe and wonder, the imagination, and "the need to be amazed." On the contrary, it will give much greater, and increasing, scope to this. It will give flight on a much grander scale to the imagination, in dialectical relation with—and in an overall sense as a part of—a systematic and comprehensive scientific outlook and method for comprehending and transforming reality.

"Materialism and Romanticism: Can We Do Without Myth?"
Observations on Art and Culture, Science and Philosophy, 2005

Supplement

"A Leap of Faith" and a Leap to Rational Knowledge: Two Very Different Kinds of Leaps, Two Radically Different Worldviews and Methods

Editor's note: The following consists of major parts of an article written by Bob Avakian in response to a letter that was sent to him via RCP Publications. In addition to attacking communism, that letter also argued against the basic scientific viewpoint and method and insisted that atheism is just another form of religion. This article responds to a number of points in that letter while focusing on the fundamental difference between a scientific outlook and method—and more particularly the scientific outlook and method of communism—on the one hand and, on the other hand, a religious worldview which relies on "leaps of faith." The article in its entirety can be found in *Revolution* #10, July 31, 2005, and is posted at revcom.us.

Not long ago I received a letter from someone who was provoked by hearing parts of my talk, "God Does Not Exist—We Need Liberation Without Gods," that were played by Michael Slate on Pacifica radio station KPFK in Los Angeles.[1] In that letter, there are many distortions....

But what I want to focus on here—because it is a very important point of distortion which not only character- izes this letter but is much more broadly promoted, par- ticularly by religious fundamentalists, and is the source of considerable confusion and misunderstanding—is the insistence that communism (and atheism generally) is actually just another form of religion and that in fact not only communism but all scientific thinking involves just as much a "leap of faith" as does religion. In this article, I will discuss how this is completely wrong and will examine the crucial differences between religion and "leaps of faith," on the one hand, and science and the scientific method—including communism, with its thor- ough, systematic and comprehensive scientific outlook and method—on the other hand.

This claim that communism (and more generally a scientific outlook and method) is just another form of religion is concentrated in the following from this letter:

"I hope you're not offended that I call your atheism faith. I'm sure you realize atheism is a faith system too. And since you've pinned you're [sic] hope on its truthfulness, we can call it your religion. How about that!? Bob Avakian is a religious man!

"You probably realize what most evolutionists don't since no one was there to record the Big Bang, it too is just as much a leap of faith as the biblical version of creation. But no worries, you can always make your case stronger by stating forcefully, 'Evolution is a fact!'"

The heart of the matter here—and what is funda- mentally wrong in the viewpoint of the writer of this letter—is the attempt to distort what is involved in the application of a scientific method and approach, in the process of scientific investigation and analysis and in the drawing of scientifically based conclusions. More specifically, what is fundamentally wrong is the attempt to say that the actual leaps that are involved in arriving at *rational knowledge of things*—including through the application of the scientific method—somehow amount to the *same thing* as "leaps of faith" that are characteristic of religion. In fact, these are profoundly and radically *different kinds* of "leaps," and digging into the difference will not only further expose the confusion and outright distortions and misrepresentations in this letter, and in the method of thinking of its author, but much more importantly can help clarify the fundamental difference between a scientific and a religious approach to reality and to changing—or not changing—reality, including human society.

The Leap From Perceptual to Rational Knowledge

As Mao Tsetung pointed out in his important philosophical works, such as "On Practice," in the gaining (or accumulation) of knowledge by people, there are two basic stages: The first is the stage of *perceptual* knowledge, and the second stage is that of *rational* knowledge. And arriving at the second stage, of rational knowledge, not only involves and requires building on what is learned through the first (perceptual) stage but also making a *leap* in *systematizing* what is perceived: identifying the "patterns" in what is perceived and the essential character and basic identity of things that lie beyond the outward appearance of things. Getting into this further, and using some examples from "everyday life" can help illustrate this fundamental point. It can make more clear the fundamental difference between the actual acquiring of rational knowledge, through a leap from perceptual knowledge to rational knowledge, and a religious "leap of faith" which does not, and cannot, lead to rational knowledge.

As Mao also pointed out, when we first encounter anything, we see it in only a partial and scattered way, observing some of its features but not what "ties them together"—what is the essential character of something, which gives to that thing its identity as such—and how it is both different from and at the same time relates to *other* things. This is the stage of simply *perceiving* something, of *perceptual* knowledge. For example, many people who are not "into football" have commented that, in looking at a game of football (on television, for example) it just appears that a lot of very bulked-up guys, wearing a lot of strange equipment, are running around and violently banging into and jumping in piles on each other! But, if you watch football for a while and persevere in attempting to grasp what is actually going on, you can begin to see the "patterns" involved, and the "rules" and "laws" that actually govern and give shape and identity to what is happening. Football fans are familiar with the basic nature and essential character of the game, with its "rules" and "laws," and can readily offer all kinds of opinions and judgements about what is going on, based on an understanding of all this. But, of course, when such fans first started watching football themselves, they were not familiar with all this and it seemed to them, too, to be a bunch of random, arbitrary and "disjointed" activity. So what is involved in moving from that to an understanding of the nature of this game and its governing "rules" and "laws" is a matter of *accumulating more and more perceptual knowledge* and then making a *leap*, "putting this together" and *systematizing* it—analyzing it and making a *synthesis* of what is at the heart of it, what are the key "patterns" involved and what "ties it all together" and gives this game its character as "football." Now, quite often this actual leap, from perceptual to rational knowledge, goes on largely unconsciously after a certain point—in many cases, the person involved is not aware of consciously making this leap to rational knowledge— but it is a real leap nonetheless and leads to a *higher form* of understanding, *rational knowledge*. (Whether it is worth it to engage in the process and effort of moving from perceptual knowledge to rational knowledge with regard to football is, of course, something that is culturally and socially influenced, and also involves matters of personal preference within that context—and I will not offer any opinions or judgements about this, one way or the other, here!)

But let's contrast this kind of leap—a leap *from perceptual to rational knowledge* of *real things*—to a "leap of faith." Let us imagine someone saying, "I don't have to watch football, or listen to explanations about it, I can come to understand it because 'god will reveal it to me.'" That would be putting forward a "leap of faith" as the way to acquire knowledge of something (in this case football). But, in fact, this kind of "leap" will not lead to actual knowledge of real things, nor can it be tested by applying means and methods that relate to the actual world of real things—there is no way to test that person's assertion that "god will reveal" this knowledge to them, there can be no evidence of this, outside of their own claim about it. But I certainly wouldn't advise you to be guided by that kind of "knowledge," supposedly arrived at through that kind of "leap of faith," if you are going to Las Vegas or Atlantic City to bet on football games!

Let's take another example: a trial in which someone is accused of robbery. The prosecutor will try to present evidence (witness testimony and/or other evidence) which shows that the defendant was at the place where the robbery occurred, at the time it occurred, and perhaps that the defendant was found in possession of a weapon that is very much like (or even identical to) the weapon used in the robbery, and so on. On the other side, the defense may try to show (through witness testimony, etc.) that the defendant was somewhere else entirely at the time the robbery occurred, and/or that the weapon the defendant was found with is in fact a *different* weapon than the one used in the robbery, and so on. When the jury moves to render a verdict, they will be called on to *make a leap* from perceptual to rational knowledge—to "sift through" the testimony and other facts and get to the *essence* of what is shown by that evidence. Of course, the jury may do this poorly—they may be influenced by prejudices, particularly against the defendant, and/or they may simply make a mistake in their attempt to determine the "patterns" and the "essential reality" of what has been presented to them—but that does not change the fact that what is required, what they are called on to do, is precisely to make a *leap* from *facts* presented (testimony, etc.) to a conclusion about *what those facts reveal that is essential about what is at issue* (whether or not the defendant committed the robbery). Once again, what is involved is a *leap* from *perceptual* knowledge to *rational* knowledge.

If, for example, the defense presents 10 witnesses, including people who have no relation to the defendant, who testify that, at the time the robbery was committed, they are *certain* that they saw the defendant in a different location entirely from where the robbery occurred—and especially if the prosecution is not able to "shake" those witnesses with regard to this testimony—then it is *only logical* to conclude that the defendant did not commit the robbery and must be found not guilty. But the important thing, in relation to the points being discussed here, is to recognize that what is involved in arriving at that verdict is "drawing a conclusion from the facts"—which again involves and requires an actual *leap* from *perceptual* knowledge (hearing the testimony) to *rational* knowledge (making the determination, drawing the conclusion, that the person could not have committed the robbery). That this is *the only logical conclusion* that could be drawn from the facts presented may tend to "blur" the fact that there is a leap involved—that reaching this conclusion requires going beyond the mere hearing of the facts to "putting the facts together" and *grasping the essence* of what those facts show. And it is important to emphasize that what is involved is precisely a *logical* conclusion—one that is arrived at by applying logical reasoning to enable the leap from perceptual to rational knowledge.

Again, let us contrast this with a "leap of faith." If someone were sitting on the jury and they said, "I know that boy is guilty because 'The Lord told me so'"—that would be the *opposite* of applying logic and reason: It would be a "leap of faith," *as opposed to* the leap from perceptual to rational knowledge—a "leap of faith" that would fly in the face of the facts and of the logical process involved in making a *radically different* kind of leap: a leap from perceptual to rational knowledge. And I don't think I have to make much of an argument that it would not be very desirable to have people on a jury who would be proceeding by making those kinds of "leaps of faith" and determining the fate of someone in that way.

Or, let's take a final example from "everyday life." If a small child observes traffic—and especially if what is involved in the flow of traffic, etc., is explained to the child by an adult—the child will come to see, before too long, that if they step out into moving traffic, they will be badly hurt, or even killed: they will have gone from seeing what at first appears to be the random movement of vehicles, without a definite "pattern" and character, to understanding what the "pattern" and the essential character of this movement of vehicles is, and when it is safe, and not safe, to cross the street. Here again what is involved is the kind of leap from perceptual to rational knowledge that we have seen illustrated in previous examples. But if the adult instructing the child were to tell them, "It is safe to walk out in front of the moving traffic, because 'god will protect you'"—that would be, not a leap from perceptual to rational knowledge, but a "leap of faith" that flies in the face of reason and logic— and would almost certainly have terrible and tragic consequences.

Scientific Knowledge and the Scientific Method

And if this crucial difference between these two radically different kinds of leaps—the leap from perceptual to rational knowledge, as opposed to a "leap of faith"— applies, and is of real importance, in "everyday life," this is so in a concentrated way with regard to scientific knowledge: knowledge that is acquired and tested through the consistent and systematic application of the scientific method—in contrast with "leaps of faith."

The scientific method involves carrying out investigations of reality, including through observation and experimentation, to accumulate facts which then are systematized into a theory which gets to what it is that these facts have in common, what *patterns* they reveal, and what is the essential character of what is involved. Then this theory is *tested* by applying it once more against the standard of what can be learned through further experimentation and observation proceeding according to this theory, to see if the results are consistently in line with what is predicted by this theory. If, in the application of this scientific method, results are obtained—things are observed or results produced through experiments, and so on—that *contradict* the theory; if, for example, things can be shown to happen which this theory predicts *could not* happen; then it must be concluded that the theory is wrong, or at least that it contains flaws (is wrong in some respects). If, however, after repeated testing, from a number of different directions and over a whole period of time, the results continue to be consistently in line with what is predicted by the theory—and no results or observations lead to facts which are in contradiction to the theory, or cannot be explained by it—then it can be concluded that this theory is correct. But, even in achieving the status of a generally accepted scientific theory, any particular theory must not only be subjected to repeated testing but it must also be subjected to review by other scientists, particularly those with knowledge and expertise in the particular field of science that the theory relates to; and if it "passes" that review—if none of these scientists can show that the theory is flawed, or simply wrong, if there are no results which can be shown to contradict the theory and its predictions about reality—then the theory will acquire general acceptance in the scientific community as a valid and true explanation of reality (or that part of reality that the theory deals with).

Now, it is true that the development of scientific theories generally involves the formulation of initial "conjectures" and "preliminary hypotheses" about things—in other words, in a sense scientists often make "informed guesses" about the way something in reality might be, even before they can provide proof of this. But, first of all, even these preliminary hypotheses are themselves based on previously accumulated, and verified, evidence about the way reality actually is—as opposed to "leaps of faith" and religious declarations about things, which we are simply expected to believe without any concrete evidence or the prospect of ever being able to obtain such evidence. Secondly, scientists take their preliminary hypotheses and systematically test them in the real world, and only on that basis are new scientific facts generated which can then contribute to the development of generally accepted scientific theories.

Of course, scientists can, do, and have made mistakes. This has happened not only with individual scientists but at times even with the scientific community in general and those who are regarded as "experts" and "authorities" in various fields of science. Scientists are after all human beings with limitations; they live in and are part of society, and they are influenced in various ways by the ideas which prevail in society at a given time. At the same time, as further knowledge is acquired—as further experimentation and observation goes on, not only in direct relation to a particular theory but in science, and indeed in the world at large—any particular theory will be subjected to continued testing and review, and it may turn out that new things that are learned call into question parts, or in some cases even all, of a particular theory, and then the theory will have to be modified or even completely discarded. *But the crucial point is this*: The scientific method provides the means for continuing to investigate reality and continuing to learn more about it, and on that basis to correct mistakes that are made.

The understanding of reality that is gained, through the leap from perceptual to rational knowledge, becomes, in turn, the basis, the foundation, from which further perceptual knowledge that is accumulated is analyzed and synthesized to make *further leaps* of this kind (from perceptual to rational knowledge yet again...and then again...). So the acquiring of knowledge—by individuals and by society and humanity overall—is not a "one-time" thing, but an ongoing process. This applies to "everyday life" and it applies in a concentrated way with regard to the conscious and systematic application of the scientific method. This relates to another point Mao emphasized: beyond the leap from perceptual knowledge to rational knowledge, there is a further leap—from rational knowledge to practice, in the course of which material reality is changed and further perceptual knowledge is gained, laying the foundation for a further leap to rational knowledge...and on...and on.

A "Leap of Faith" is a Leap Away From a True Understanding of Reality

In opposition to this, a religious worldview—which insists on a reliance on faith and "leaps of faith" instead of investigation and analysis of the real world and the leap from perceptual to rational knowledge—such a religious worldview cannot lead to a true understanding of reality, and in fact is bound to lead away from such an understanding in fundamental ways. Of course, not all people who are religious are "scriptural literalists"—who insist on an acceptance of the Bible (or some other scripture of some other religion) as the declared word of a supposed all-powerful and all-knowing supernatural being and therefore the "absolute truth." In fact, there are many religious people who accept a good deal of the conclusions of science, and there are more than a few who try to reconcile their belief in some kind of supernatural being with an acceptance of the scientific method and its results, as applied to the realm of material existence. At the same time, however, their religious viewpoint insists that there is some other realm, of non-material existence, when in fact there is not; and there has never been and could not be evidence offered for the existence of this non-material realm which could meet the test of scientific investigation. And it is a fact that even those who attempt to reconcile religious belief, of one kind or another, with a general acceptance of the scientific method and the results of applying this method, *cannot consistently do so*, because those religious beliefs are bound to conflict, at certain times and in certain ways, with the conclusions reached by the application of the scientific method.

The Big Bang, Evolution, and Revolution

Let's return to a core argument of this letter, as expressed in the part I quoted above. Let's take what has been said here—contrasting the scientific method with a religious worldview, and contrasting in particular the leap from perceptual to rational knowledge with "leaps of faith"—and apply this to examples the writer of this letter emphasizes: *evolution* and the *Big Bang*. It is a fact that evolution and the Big Bang have in common that they are scientific theories that provide explanation for fundamental aspects of the development of the known universe (the universe that is known to human beings) and of our earth and the living things, including human beings, on this earth. (In very basic terms, the Big Bang theory says that the universe, as we know it today, including our earth, originated with a cataclysmic [sudden and violent] explosion of matter billions of years ago.) At the same time, while there is substantial scientific evidence supporting the theory of the Big Bang, the theory of evolution is even more firmly established and has been confirmed by over 150 years of scientific testing and review, since the time that Charles Darwin first systematized the theory of evolution in the 19th century. This includes the understanding that human beings evolved out of a long succession of life-forms that have evolved over several billion years, and it includes clear evidence that human beings and the great apes are closely related biologically, and that in fact they shared common ancestor species from which they diverged along separate evolutionary paths only a few million years ago. The very important series *The Science of Evolution*, by Ardea Skybreak, which appeared in our Party's newspaper (and which I understand will be published in the not-too-distant future as a book by Insight Press[2]), provides a thorough explanation of the theory of evolution and how it has been demonstrated—repeatedly, from many different directions, and by the application of the scientific method in many different fields—to be true; how continuing scientific investigation and summation, from many different fields of science (including genetics as well as the fossil record and many other "fields of scientific inquiry") continue to validate and provide further evidence for evolution; how there has not ever been a single scientific discovery or verified fact which in any way would disprove evolution or call it into question; how, in sum, evolution is one of the most well-established and fundamental theories in all of science, one of the most fundamental components of a true understanding of reality. And *The Science of Evolution* also thoroughly exposes and refutes attempts by religious fundamentalists and some others to call evolution into question or to challenge its fundamental truths, through putting forward literal Biblical "Creationism" or "more sophisticated" distortions of reality, such as "Intelligent Design," which is in fact another variant of "Creationism."

With this in mind, let's look at the claim by the writer of this letter that evolution, no less than the Big Bang, is "just as much a leap of faith as the biblical version of creation." From all that has been said so far, it should be clear that this statement is utterly and completely false. Evolution has been shown to be true and has been continually further verified, *by application of the scientific method*—which, again, *involves* definite *leaps from perceptual to rational knowledge* but involves *nothing* of a "leap of faith." In fact, "leaps of faith" are alien to, and are in direct conflict with and violation of, the scientific method—and if it can be shown that, as opposed to a logical leap from perceptual to rational knowledge, a scientific theory actually involved "a leap of faith" which by definition could not be substantiated, or even tested, by scientific methods, *that theory would immediately be understood to be invalid according to the standards of science and the scientific method*. There are no "leaps of faith" in the scientific method, and there is no "leap of faith" in the theory of evolution; its findings and the means by which they have been arrived at (and are continually being further verified and validated), are in direct opposition to "leaps of faith" and to the notion of an understanding of reality that relies on such "leaps of faith" and on "faith" as some kind of means for arriving at the truth about reality. Therefore, when I (and, more significantly for this discussion, the overwhelming, overwhelming majority of scientists in the field of biology and more generally people in the scientific community) declare, without hesitation, that "Evolution is a fact!"—this may annoy the writer of this letter and upset his religious prejudices, but that does not make it any less true that evolution is, indeed, a fact.

And by now it should also be clear what is fundamentally wrong with the comment by the writer of this letter that, "since no one was there to record the Big Bang, it too is just as much a leap of faith as the biblical version of creation." While (at least to my understanding) the Big Bang, as a scientific theory, is not as well substantiated and verified as evolution—and while there is definitely much more to be learned about the origins and developments of the universe (or perhaps many different universes), and people in the field of physics (or other sciences) would be the first to say this—it is not at all the case that the theory of the Big Bang is just as much a matter of a "leap of religious faith" as the myth of biblical creation. First of all, the story of creation, as told in the book of Genesis in the Bible, is simply wrong—it is clearly contradicted by many scientifically established facts in many particular details and in its overall presentation—not the least of which is the fact that it can be shown, scientifically, that the earth is billions of years old, not a few thousand years old, that the earth revolves around the sun, and that many other forms of plant and animal species existed long before human beings first appeared on earth. In opposition to this biblical creation myth, while (again, to my understanding) the Big Bang theory has not been as thoroughly verified by scientific methods as evolution has, it is certainly not the case that the Big Bang theory is, at this point at least, contradicted, in its main features, by scientific understanding and by results arrived at through the scientific method—as, again, is *definitely the case with the biblically based myth of creation.*

It is of course true that no human being was around at the time of the Big Bang. But this does not invalidate the Big Bang theory or reduce it to "an article of faith" like the biblically based myth of creation. Human beings come to know many things about reality which we do not directly experience or witness. The Big Bang theory has in fact been formulated and developed through a process (which is ongoing) of *proceeding from things that have already been clearly established and demonstrated, from many directions, to be true,* and "putting these things together" to draw a conclusion about the larger reality that these things are part of. In other words, there is indeed a leap involved here—but, once again, it is not a "leap of faith," or anything like it, but *a leap from evidence to a conclusion about what the evidence shows to be true.*

In short, in developing the Big Bang theory, scientists in the fields of astronomy and physics, and other fields, have proceeded from what they do know—what has been scientifically established and tested and verified—about the universe to draw further inferences and conclusions about the universe, including its origins. And at every stage in the development of this scientific theory (as in all scientific theories), these inferences and conclusions have to be, and are, subjected to further testing in reality before they can be raised to the level of a verified theory and gain general acceptance. The Big Bang theory is a work in progress, but it is not idle speculation: the very questions it poses and explores, the research it stimulates, and the concrete facts it has so far helped to uncover are based on previously accumulated scientific evidence about reality. And this once again marks a profound difference between the scientific method and "religious faith"—since the latter, by definition, does not draw its conclusions, or make its assertions, based on a scientific investigation of and summation of actual reality and *cannot, by definition*, be tested by scientific methods. In contrast to the biblical creation story of the origin of the universe, the fact is that the Big Bang theory is being continually subjected to further scientific "probing" and analysis. Even though it is true that no human being was present at the time that scientists have calculated that the Big Bang occurred (about 15 billion years ago) the development of new technology—including more powerful telescopes and related instruments, which can be sent into space to record things—has enabled scientists to learn much more about what happened at a time which was shortly after the time when the Big Bang is believed to have occurred, at a point in space far from where our earth now exists. ("Shortly" in this context means something like a billion years, which is not that great a time span in the context of the universe and its development. The reason that scientists are able, in this way, to "see far into the past" in the universe's development has to do with the relation between time and space. Since things that are observed by human beings—directly or with the aid of telescopes and similar instruments—are "transmitted" to us through the medium of light, and at the speed of light, things that occurred long ago but also a long distance from the observer take a long time to reach the observer, even though the speed of light is very fast compared to other everyday movements we are familiar with. For example, if you are in a thunderstorm, you will see a lightning bolt before you hear the thunder connected with it, even though the two actually are part of one phenomenon and actually occurred at the same time. The reason you see the lightning first is that lightning travels at the speed of *light*, which is much faster than the speed of *sound* which brings the noise of the thunder.)

What scientists have learned through this "looking back in time," getting ever closer to the time when the Big Bang is believed to have occurred, has tended to substantiate (to back up and further confirm) the Big Bang theory, even while it has raised new questions relating to all this. But once more the crucial fact here, in relation to what is raised by the writer of this letter—and, more importantly, in relation to fundamental questions concerning what is truth and how human beings arrive at knowledge of the truth, and test that knowledge—is that *in no way does this increasing knowledge relating to the origins of the known universe have anything to do with the application of religious principles or "leaps of faith."* In fact, once again this increasing knowledge—arrived at through scientific methods and logical leaps from perceptual to rational knowledge that are consistent with and part of the scientific method—is *in contradiction to*, and *refutes* the biblically based myth of creation, further providing evidence that it is exactly that: a *myth*, invented several thousand years ago, by human beings who lacked knowledge of how the universe (as we know it), the earth, and the living things on the earth (including human beings) *actually* came into being.

*****

Knowing about actual reality—and continually learning more about it—is vitally important for humanity and its future; it is vitally important not only for people in the sciences and the academic world but for the brutally oppressed and exploited people of the earth, who must and can be the backbone and driving force of a revolution to throw off and put an end to all forms of exploitation and oppression, throughout the globe—to be the emancipators not only of themselves but ultimately of all humanity. Confronting reality as it actually is—and as it is changing and developing—and understanding the underlying and driving forces in this, is crucial in order to play a decisive and leading role in bringing about this revolution and ushering in a whole new era in human history, which will shatter and remove forever not only the material chains—the economic, social and political shackles of exploitation and oppression—that enslave people in today's world but also the mental chains, the ways of thinking and the culture, that correspond to and reinforce those material chains. In the Communist Manifesto, Karl Marx and Frederick Engels, who founded the communist movement over 150 years ago, declared that the communist revolution, and its emancipating principles, methods, and aims, involves a "radical rupture" not only with the traditional property relations that enslave people, in one form or another, but also a radical rupture with all traditional ideas that reflect and reinforce those traditional property relations.

The struggle in the realm of *epistemology*—the theory of knowledge and how it is acquired by people, the theory of what is true and how people come to know the truth—is a crucial arena in the overall battle for the emancipation of the oppressed and exploited majority of humanity, and ultimately of humanity as a whole. Grasping the defining characteristics and the importance of the scientific method—and, most of all, the most consistent, systematic and comprehensive scientific approach to reality, *the communist world outlook and method*, which can embrace without replacing or suffocating the many fields of human knowledge and endeavor and can give expression to the richest process of learning about reality and transforming it in the interests of humanity—is of vital importance for this emancipatory struggle. Understanding the profound difference between the attempt to impose "faith-based" notions *on* reality and, in opposition to that, pursuing a scientific understanding *of* reality, including of religion and its origins and effects—understanding the radical difference between "leaps of faith" and the ongoing acquisition of knowledge through continual leaps from perceptual knowledge to rational knowledge—this is a crucial part of carrying forward the struggle to achieve the two radical ruptures that mark the communist revolution as the leap to a whole new, liberating era in human history.

Notes:

1. Audio files of the talk "God Does Not Exist—We Need Liberation Without Gods" are available online at bobavakian.net.

2. This series has now been published as a book: Ardea Skybreak, *The Science of Evolution and the Myth of Creationism—Knowing What's Real and Why It Matters*, Insight Press, 2006.

CHAPTER 5
MORALITY, REVOLUTION AND THE GOAL OF COMMUNISM

#1

The basis for communist morality is contained, in a concentrated way, in what Maoists refer to as the "4 Alls." This is drawn from the summary by Marx of what the communist revolution aims for and leads to: the abolition of all class distinctions (or "class distinctions generally"); the abolition of all the relations of production on which these class distinctions rest; the abolition of all the social relations that correspond to these relations of production; and the revolutionizing of all the ideas that result from these social relations. (See *The Class Struggles in France, 1848 to 1850.*)

> *Preaching from a Pulpit of Bones, We Need Morality*
> *But Not* Traditional *Morality,* 1999

#2

One of the main accusations from those who oppose communism is that communists believe "the ends justify the means"—that anything is permissible so long as it can be said to be helping to move things toward the attainment of communism, eventually. This is not only untrue, it is an inversion of the truth. It is a principle of communism that the means must be *consistent with* and must flow from the ends (or aims). It is often necessary, and desirable, for communists to struggle for goals that are short of the final aim represented by the "4 Alls"—since this can contribute to the ultimate achievement of those "4 Alls"—but it is never acceptable for communists to uphold or fight for things, or to use means and methods, that are in *basic opposition* to that final aim. Communism demands the most determined and daring search for the truth, even if that truth should make one uncomfortable in the short run, because the more one grasps the truth—the more one has a correct and as comprehensive as possible an understanding of objective reality—the more possible it is to transform objective reality in a direction that best serves the interests of humanity.

Preaching from a Pulpit of Bones

#3

The whole point of principle is that you have to fight for it when it is not easy to do. There is no need for principle if the only time it is applied is when it doesn't matter.

"Methods and Principles,"
Observations on Art and Culture, Science and Philosophy, 2005

#4

"Western morality"—and, for that matter, the dominant morality in all parts of the world, wherever society is marked by class division and exploitation, patriarchy, and other forms of oppression—has always been a rationale and justification for oppression.

Preaching from a Pulpit of Bones

#5

The "Bible Belt" in the U.S. is also the Lynching Belt.

Away With All Gods! Unchaining the Mind and Radically Changing the World, 2008

#6

Editor's note: Here Bob Avakian talks about the 1960s.

Between the anti-war protesters and the war planners in the Pentagon; between the Black Panthers and J. Edgar Hoover; between Black, Latino, Asian, and Native peoples on the one side and the government on the other; between the women who rebelled against their "traditional" roles and the rich old men who ruled the country; between the youth who brought forward new music, in the broadest sense, and the preachers who denounced them as disciples of the devil and despoilers of civilization: the battle lines were sharply drawn. And through the course of those tumultuous times, those who were rebelling against the established order and the dominating relations and traditions increasingly found common cause and powerful unity; they increasingly gained—and deserved—the moral as well as political initiative, while the ruling class dug in and lashed out to defend its rule, but increasingly, and very deservedly, lost moral and political authority.

Preaching from a Pulpit of Bones

#7

American Lives Are *Not* More Important Than Other People's Lives.

Bringing Forward Another Way, Revolution #88, May 13, 2007

#8

Internationalism—The Whole World Comes First.

Bullets, From the Writings, Speeches, & Interviews of Bob Avakian, Chairman of the Revolutionary Communist Party, USA, 1985

#9

We have to win people to be communists, and then actively take up the process of recruiting them. We need to recruit *communists*, people who are prepared and determined to dedicate their lives to revolution and the final aim of a communist world—to being emancipators of humanity—to contributing as much as they can, in an organized and disciplined way, to that cause.

Making Revolution and Emancipating Humanity – Part 2: "Everything We're Doing Is About Revolution," Revolution #116, January 20, 2008

#10

Here I want to bring up a formulation that I love, because it captures so much that is essential. Soon after September 11, someone said, or wrote somewhere, that living in the U.S. is a little bit like living in the house of Tony Soprano. You know, or you have a sense, that all the goodies that you've gotten have something to do with what the master of the house is doing out there in the world. Yet you don't want to look too deeply or too far at what that might be, because it might upset everything—not only what you have, all your possessions, but all the assumptions on which you base your life.

Bringing Forward Another Way, Revolution #87, May 6, 2007

#11

There is a place where epistemology and morality meet. There is a place where you have to stand and say: It is not acceptable to refuse to look at something—or to refuse to believe something—because it makes you uncomfortable. And: It is not acceptable to believe something just because it makes you feel comfortable.

Bringing Forward Another Way, Revolution #87, May 6, 2007

#12

After the Holocaust, the worst thing that has happened to Jewish people is the state of Israel.

Revolution #63, October 1, 2006

#13

The fact remains that your life, whether shorter or longer (within this overall finite framework), is going to be devoted to one kind of objective or another. It is going to be shaped by larger forces that are independent of your will, but then there is the question of how, yes, each individual—as well as in a different, larger dimension, social classes—respond to the way in which the contradictions that are shaping things confront and impinge on them. And there is conscious volition and conscious decision in terms of what people do with their lives, in relation to what they see as necessary, possible, and desirable.

Ruminations and Wranglings: On the Importance of
Marxist Materialism, Communism as a Science,
Meaningful Revolutionary Work, and a Life with Meaning,
Revolution #164, May 17, 2009

#14

Religion is the doctrine of submission—blind obedience; Marxism of rebellion—ever more conscious rebellion.

Communists Are Rebels: A Letter from
RCP Chairman Bob Avakian to His Parents on Philosophy,
Religion, Morals, and Continuous Revolution, 1980

#15

"Never underestimate the great importance of ideology."

We have a very negative example of this with the Islamic fundamentalists. The way in which they are proceeding to do what they're doing has a very powerful ideological component to it.

How do people respond to the conditions that they
find themselves in? What course or road do they take,
and what do they respond to, in the face of those
conditions? This is not predetermined. There is not
just one way that people respond, automatically and
regardless of influences on them. And even the level
on which people sacrifice depends on their ideological
orientation to a very significant degree.

Bringing Forward Another Way, Revolution #98, August 19, 2007

#16

Let us be clear: female children, and children
in general, should not be seen and treated as
the property of their parents, and their father in
particular. That is not the world we are aiming
for, not a world worth living in. This is the way it
has been for thousands of years, and this has been
embodied in and promoted by religious scripture
and tradition, but this is not how we want the world
to be, and not how it needs to be. Yes, children need
discipline. But they don't need to be beaten with
a switch or a rod in order to be disciplined, and
to have a sense of purpose. They need to be led—
inspired, and yes, at times, taken firmly in hand—as
part of an overall vision and goal of bringing into
being a radically different and much better world.
And, as they become older and more conscious of
this objective, and capable of acting consciously to

contribute to it, they can increasingly become a part
of that process. But even before they are capable
of being consciously a part of this, the principles
that apply to bringing such a world into being
should apply, in a fundamental sense, in relating to
children—your own and others.

Away With All Gods!

#17

It is necessary to be boldly saying to people: "We don't
need the church, we don't need the switch, we don't
need the rod, and, no, we don't need the gangs and the
drugs—**we need revolution.**"

Away With All Gods!

#18

In many ways, and particularly for men, the woman
question and whether you seek to completely abolish
or to preserve the existing property and social
relations and corresponding ideology that enslave
women (or maybe "just a little bit" of them) is a
touchstone question *among the oppressed themselves.*
It is a dividing line between "wanting in" and really
"wanting out": between fighting to end all oppression
and exploitation—and the very division of society into
classes—and seeking in the final analysis to get your
part in this.

Revolution #158, March 8, 2009
(quote originally published 1984)

#19

While, again, there is certainly more to be learned about this, it can be said that, with regard to the sphere of sexuality, in some significant ways for the communist movement overall, and specifically for our party...the question of homosexuality has been emblematic of the weakness of the communist movement and socialist states historically—from the time of Engels, with his unfortunate remarks denigrating homosexuality, up through the Chinese revolution. This, in a significant way, has concentrated a weakness of the communist movement on the question of sexuality more generally, including specifically how this relates to the status, and the struggle for the complete liberation, of women....

The Need and the Basis for a Further Leap and Radical Rupture

So, while again there is definitely more to be learned through further investigation, study, analysis and synthesis, all this does, I believe, establish that there is a need for a further radical rupture, to lay a firmer foundation for really achieving the "4 Alls" in their fullest dimension. This has not been given full expression or been fully recognized in the history of the communist movement, including in the history of our party, until very recently when we have begun to seriously address questions from a different and much more radical standpoint.

The change in the position of our party on the question of

homosexuality [to one which fully supports the struggle against the oppression of gay people as an important part of advancing toward the goal of communism and the emancipation of all humanity]* is, in very significant measure, a result of what has developed into the New Synthesis, and specifically the method and approach embodied in that New Synthesis. It represents a breaking with a lot of trends and tendencies within the communist movement which, to no small degree, have been suffocating of the kind of radical theory and radical movement that communism actually should be and must be. But, in a real sense, this constitutes a beginning, which we need to build on and go much further with—on the basis of a scientific approach and the scientific synthesis of what I referred to earlier as the visceral and the theoretical.

Unresolved Contradictions, Driving Forces for Revolution – Part III: "The New Synthesis and the Woman Question: The Emancipation of Women and the Communist Revolution – Further Leaps and Radical Ruptures," *Revolution* #196, March 28, 2010

* Until the late 1990s, the Revolutionary Communist Party, while opposing discrimination based on sexual orientation, regarded homosexuality as a negative social phenomenon, and something which should be struggled against ideologically, in a way similar to religion. In the latter part of the 1990s, as an important part of making further radical ruptures with certain backward views and political positions which actually embodied aspects of "tradition's chains"—including within the international communist movement historically—the RCP began a process of study and analysis, which led to a fundamental change in its position on this question. For a basic statement on this change in position, and the process of critical examination and analysis which led to this change, see "On the Position on Homosexuality in the New Draft Programme," published by the RCP in 2001.

#20

The situation cannot be allowed to continue where the
alternatives with major social impact within this society
are self-indulgent individualism, on the one hand,
or, on the other hand, religious fundamentalism and
subordination and sacrifice of the self to the collective
juggernaut of imperialist conquest and plunder, as for
example in the U.S. military; and where, in one form
or another, a culture and morality serving the interests
of the most monstrous exploiters and oppressors—and
a system which does indeed, without the slightest bit
of exaggeration, crush lives and mangle spirits on a
massive scale, throughout the world, while having
the audacity to present itself as the best of all possible
systems and a shining example for the world—has
virtually unchallenged hegemony.

The point is that there is a real need and a real basis
to be bringing forward, fighting for—and, yes, living,
even now—a radically different philosophy and a
radically different culture and morality. And besides
the realms of culture and morality there is a need, as
has been emphasized before, for a fierce battle in the
ideological/epistemological realm, particularly against
relativism and its pernicious effects. Again, we see
now a situation that is too much like that described in
the poem by William Butler Yeats: "The worst are full
of passionate intensity"—and absolutist certainty, we

might add—while "the best lack all conviction." This has to be radically taken on and radically changed.

Birds Cannot Give Birth to Crocodiles,
But Humanity Can Soar Beyond the Horizon – Part 2:
"Building the Movement for Revolution," *Revolution*, 2011

#21

Do Black people need to take responsibility? Responsibility for what?

Responsibility for *REVOLUTION*—DEFINITELY! We all need to take responsibility for making revolution—to emancipate all of humanity from this whole system of oppression.

"In the Wake of the Election, a Basic Point of Orientation: To the Masses…With Revolution," *Revolution* #149, November 30, 2008

#22

The death of Willie "Mobile" Shaw* is a terrible and bitter loss. Willie wanted his life to be about something—something beyond the dog-eat-dog and the murderous madness this system brings down on people, and catches them up in, in a thousand ways every day. He joined the revolution, became a communist and dedicated his life to the liberation of all people who are oppressed by this system—not just people of one race, or in one neighborhood, but men and women of all races, nations, and languages, all over the world. Most of them Willie had never met, but he came to see that they shared a common fate and could bring a much better future into being. Willie's life is proof that those this rotten system tries in every way to drag down—can rise up; that those the system treats as less than human—can become the liberators of all humanity.

Willie never turned his back on people who had not yet come to see the world as he had come to see it—as it really is; he never gave up on winning them to the fight for a radically different and much better world. Willie brought to the revolution a gigantic heart, a wealth of life experience and great wisdom drawn from that experience. I consider myself very fortunate to have met Willie and spent time talking with him. He asked me many questions—and he helped me learn many things. Willie said to me: "You are the only hope we have." I have kept those words in my heart, with a deep sense of responsibility to live up to them. But Willie, and all the people like Willie in the world, are also the ones who give *me* hope—they represent the hope of humanity for a better world. Willie's whole life experience, and his all too early death, cry out the need for revolution. And the changes Willie went through, in his all too short life—the way he came through so much to take up the cause of liberating humanity—shout out the *possibility* of revolution. As our hearts ache over the loss of Willie, let us keep in our hearts, and let us learn all we can, from the beautiful human being that Willie "Mobile" Shaw was and the way in which, in dedicating his life to revolution and communism, he truly made it count, in the greatest way possible.

> "Statement by Bob Avakian, Chairman of the Revolutionary Communist Party, on the Occasion of the Death of Willie 'Mobile' Shaw," *Revolution* #27, December 18, 2005

* Willie "Mobile" Shaw grew up and lived his whole life in the Nickerson Gardens Housing Project in Watts, Los Angeles. After working with revolutionaries there for a period of time, he joined the Revolutionary Communist Party, USA. The hardship of his life conditions led to his having a serious illness, and he died on November 24, 2005 due to complications following surgery.

#23

If you have had a chance to see the world as it really is, there are profoundly different roads you can take with your life. You can just get into the dog-eat-dog, and most likely get swallowed up by that while trying to get ahead in it. You can put your snout into the trough and try to scarf up as much as you can, while scrambling desperately to get more than others. Or you can try to do something that would change the whole direction of society and the whole way the world is. When you put those things alongside each other, which one has any meaning, which one really contributes to anything worthwhile? Your life is going to be about something— or it's going to be about nothing. And there is nothing greater your life can be about than contributing whatever you can to the revolutionary transformation

of society and the world, to put an end to all systems
and relations of oppression and exploitation and all
the unnecessary suffering and destruction that goes
along with them. I have learned that more and more
deeply through all the twists and turns and even the
great setbacks, as well as the great achievements, of the
communist revolution so far, in what are really still its
early stages historically.

*From Ike to Mao and Beyond: My Journey from Mainstream America
to Revolutionary Communist, A Memoir by Bob Avakian, 2005*

#24

In the final analysis, as Engels once expressed it, the
proletariat must win its emancipation on the battlefield.
But there is not only the question of winning in this
sense but of how we win in the largest sense. One of
the significant if perhaps subtle and often little-noticed
ways in which the enemy, even in defeat, seeks to
exact revenge on the revolution and sow the seeds
of its future undoing is in what he would force the
revolutionaries to become in order to defeat him. It will
come to this: we will have to face him in the trenches
and defeat him amidst terrible destruction but we
must not in the process annihilate the fundamental
difference between the enemy and ourselves. Here the
example of Marx is illuminating: he repeatedly fought
at close quarters with the ideologists and apologists
of the bourgeoisie but he never fought them on their

terms or with their outlook; with Marx his method is as exhilarating as his goal is inspiring. We must be able to maintain our firmness of principles but at the same time our flexibility, our materialism and our dialectics, our realism and our romanticism, our solemn sense of purpose and our sense of humor.

For a Harvest of Dragons: On the "Crisis of Marxism" and the Power of Marxism – Now More Than Ever, 1983

Supplement

Beyond the Narrow Horizon
of Bourgeois Right

Editor's note: The following is an excerpt from Part 1 of
Bob Avakian's talk *Making Revolution and Emancipating
Humanity* (available at revcom.us). It speaks to key principles
concerning the morality and outlook, as well as the goals, of
communism.

I want to begin by returning to a point that we continue to speak to—and for very good reasons—both
because of its great importance and because it is still so
little grasped and acted upon. This is the whole question
of getting beyond the present narrow horizons imposed
on society and on people and their thinking. Now, I am
aware that in his latest CD, *Modern Times*, Bob Dylan has
a song "Beyond the Horizon." But what we are talking
about is something entirely and radically different—it is
the narrow horizon of bourgeois right, and the need for
humanity to leap beyond *that* horizon.

"I Want to Get More"—or We Want Another World?

I was moved, or provoked, to speak to this again
in reading some reports recounting the responses of
different people, youth in particular, to watching the

DVD of my 2003 talk *Revolution: Why It's Necessary, Why It's Possible, What It's All About.* I want to begin with a comment of one youth (I believe it was a high school student in Oakland) who watched this DVD, and said he really liked it—"I agree with everything in there, and I really liked the vision of the future society"—*but*, he went on, "if I invent something, I want to get more for it."

Here we come right up against the question of making (or not making) a leap beyond the narrow horizon of bourgeois right. What do we mean by "bourgeois right"? This refers to the concept of "right" which essentially corresponds to *commodity relations*—relations in which people confront each other as owners (or non-owners) of *things* which are to be exchanged—and more specifically, relations in which the *appearance of equality* covers over profound *in*equalities, relations which are grounded in the exploitation and oppression of the many by a relative handful. In its most fundamental terms, this is grounded in a relationship where a small number of people dominate ownership not only of the wealth of society, but more fundamentally the means to produce wealth (land, raw materials, technology of various kinds, and so on), and a large number of people own little or none of these things, and so must sell their ability to work to those who do own them (and, if they are not able to sell their ability to work—if they cannot get a job—they will either starve or be forced into other means, often illegal means, in order to be able to live). Once again, this exchange—of the ability to work (or "labor power") for a wage (or salary)—*appears* to be an equal exchange; but in reality it involves and embodies a *profoundly unequal* relation, in which those without capital are forced into a subordinate position: forced to work for—and, in the process of working, creating more wealth for—those who do own and control capital.

This fundamental relation of inequality, of domination and exploitation, is extended into and embodied in all the relations of capitalist society. Take, for example, the concept of "equality before the law." This is supposed to mean that the same laws are applied, in the same ways, to everyone, regardless of what their "station" in life is, how much money they have, and so on. Experience shows, however, that this is not how things work out in reality. People with more money have more political influence—and those with a great deal of money have a great deal of political influence and power—while those with less money, and especially those with very little, also have no significant political influence, connections with political power, and so on. And this plays out, repeatedly, in legal proceedings, right down to the way in which those presiding over legal procedures (judges) look—very differently—at different kinds of people who become involved in legal proceedings. But what is even more decisive is the reality that the *laws themselves* (and the Constitution which sets the basis for the laws) *reflect and reinforce the essential relations in society*, and most fundamentally the economic (production) relations of capitalism. This, for example, is why it is perfectly legal for capitalists to lay off thousands of people, or to refuse to hire them in the first place, if these capitalists cannot make sufficient profit by employing (and exploiting) them—or if they can make more profit by employing, and exploiting, people in some other place—but it is *illegal* for people who have been denied employment in this way to take the things they need without paying for them (without giving money in exchange for these things—money which in fact they do not have, money they cannot earn, because they have been *prevented* from working, by means that are *perfectly legal* under this system). All this—and the many ways in which this finds expression in society, in the relations between groups and individuals, in the laws and institutions, and in the thinking of people— is what is meant in referring to "bourgeois right."

To dig further into what this means, let's return to the example of someone "wanting more" if they invent something. This is hardly an uncommon view. It is "spontaneous" thinking that is very common when living in a society like this, where everything is ultimately—and very often not so ultimately—measured in the very narrow, constricting terms of the cash nexus and gets expressed crudely in "what's in it for me?" So this youth could see the sweep of all that is presented in that Revolution talk, and agree with it—but, then, there was one little sticking point: "If I do something special, I want something in exchange for it, I want the chance to get something more for me."

Well, we have to examine: How do things actually work when and where people "get more"? And, for that matter, how do things actually work when and where people invent something in the first place? What is it that happens most of the time when someone invents something, and then someone ends up "getting more out of it"? Usually, it's not the person who does the inventing who "gets more"—or gets most of the profit—from this, but instead the people who have control of capital and who can turn the invention into a commodity and into capital. Because that's what has to happen in order for someone to get more out of something that is invented: there have to be the social relations, and ultimately and fundamentally the production relations, which enable that, which make it possible to turn that invention into "intellectual property"—into a commodity and into capital.

Well, in order for that to happen, there must be a whole network of capitalist relations. Otherwise, on what basis are you going to get anything—and, specifically, get more than others—if there is not a whole network of commodity relations and of capital which is undergirding and is the basis on which the whole society is functioning? And this whole network of commodity relations, and of capital, is in reality a network of *exploitation*. *That* is what has to be in operation in order for someone—and most likely *not* the inventor, but a class of people, a class of capitalists (and particular capitalists in particular instances)—to get more out of it. It is those who already control large amounts of capital, and who have a dominant position in the capitalist economy, who are most likely to benefit the most—to get more than others.

And what happens if we have a whole network of capitalist relations? What kind of world do we then have? We have the same world that's being dissected and indicted in the Revolution talk on the DVD—the same world that drove this person to say, in the first place, "I really liked what is said in that talk." You don't like this world. But if you don't want this world, then you cannot want the things that define this world and that are the underlying and driving forces in this world. You cannot want a network of commodity relations and of capital, because then you have everything that goes along with that, not only immediately around you, but throughout the world, and all the horrors that we know about and could catalog almost endlessly.

To paraphrase Lenin, capitalism puts into the hands of individuals, as individual wealth and capital, that which has been *produced by all of society*. Production under capitalism—and the turning of an invention into something which not only has use value but exchange value, which can summon money back and even "surplus value," more money than at the start of the process—requires a social production process which ends up with the surplus value (the wealth that's produced as capital) going into the hands of individuals—and a relative handful of individuals, at that. This is the point Lenin was making when he said that capitalism puts into the hands of individuals, as individual wealth and capital, that which has been produced by all of society—and today, more than ever, this takes place on a worldwide scale. After all, capital is not something neutral, and it is not wealth in some abstract sense—divorced and abstracted from the social production relations through which that wealth is produced—capital is a *social relation* in which some have *command over the labor power (the ability to work) of others* and accumulate wealth for themselves by utilizing that labor power of *others*.

Lenin added that capitalism forces people to calculate, with the stinginess of a miser, how much more they're getting than somebody else. Put that—and everything that's bound up with that, all the horrors that go along with that—up against what it would mean to *move beyond* all that, to get beyond these production relations, and the corresponding social relations, and all the conditions that are bound up with them and intertwined with them. And, further, in the situation where humanity had finally managed to throw off all this, and all the horrors that go along with it, the orientation of "wanting more for myself" would very quickly move things *backward*, in the direction of the capitalist system, with all its very real horrors. There is no other way in which ultimately and fundamentally certain individuals can "get more"—no way other than to have a whole network of relations that makes that possible, with everything that goes along with that.

Does this mean—as is often claimed by people attacking and slandering communism—that in communist society everybody will have exactly the same amount of things, regardless of their particular situation and their particular needs? No, the slogan of communism—the principle that will be applied in communist society—is precisely **from each according to their ability, to each according to their needs**. In other words, people will contribute what they can to society and will get back what they need to meet the requirements of a decent and fulfilling life, intellectually and culturally, as well as materially, on an ever expanding basis. This will involve and require a whole different outlook and morality, along with radically different economic, social, and political relations, in which it will no longer be the case that a relatively small group dominates and exploits masses of people and in which it is presented as "right and natural" for some people to have a superior position over others.

Look at that present reality, and the principles and morals that go along with it—where everyone is pushed into trying to "get more" than others, and where a small number "get much more" than the great majority—and contrast that with the much more lofty and liberating principle of **from each according to their ability, to each according to their needs**—where we move beyond the narrow horizon of bourgeois right—of "what's in it for me, what do I get," in accordance with the commodities and, in many cases, the capital that *I* have been able to accumulate through this process. This, once again, is not a neutral process, but a process of degrading and brutalizing exploitation and oppression—and today this involves exploitation and oppression of literally billions of people throughout the world, including huge numbers of children. *This* is the foundation of the present system, the capitalist-imperialist system—this is the *reality* of life under this system—in which it is a driving principle to "get more."

Again let's pose the basic question: Which is a much more liberating and lofty vision of society, and which would make a better world—this system, with its fundamental relations, and the corresponding ideas, or one in which people are receiving according to their needs while contributing according to their abilities—not on the basis of what they are going to get back out of it, in some narrow sense, but on the basis of understanding that society as a whole, including the flourishing of the individuals who make up society, is going to be on a much better foundation and reach to much greater heights if that whole orientation of "what do I get out of it" has been moved beyond, together with moving beyond the material basis for that and the necessity that is bound up with that?

This is a point we're going to have to continually struggle with people about. What kind of world do you want to live in? Do you want all the things that now characterize the world? We can go down the list of them: the oppression of women, racism and national oppression, exploitation of little children, despoliation of the environment, the wars fought in which the people on the bottom are dragged into them as the cannon fodder (as the old saying goes)...and on and on and on. Is that the world you want, so that maybe—and very unlikely—*you* might be able to "get more"? Certainly most people will not "get more." Or do you want a world free of and beyond all that, beyond the narrow horizon of bourgeois right?

CHAPTER 6
REVOLUTIONARY RESPONSIBILITY AND LEADERSHIP

#1

Lenin's argument in *What Is To Be Done?*—that the more highly organized and centralized the party was, the more it was a real vanguard organization of revolutionaries, the greater would be the role and initiative of the masses in revolutionary struggle—was powerfully demonstrated in the Russian Revolution itself and has been in all proletarian revolutions. Nowhere has such a revolution been made without such a party and nowhere has the lack of such a party contributed to unleashing the initiative of masses of the oppressed in *conscious revolutionary struggle.*

For a Harvest of Dragons: On the "Crisis of Marxism" and the Power of Marxism – Now More Than Ever, 1983

#2

What kind of organization you see as necessary depends on what you're trying to do. If all you're trying to do is make a few reforms, if you're not trying to really confront and deal with this whole system, if you're not trying to make revolution and transform society and the world, then you don't need this kind of vanguard party.

Reaching for the Heights and Flying Without a Safety Net, Revolutionary Worker #1198, May 11, 2003

#3

I have several times noted the fact that for the advanced forces, for those who come to the forefront of the revolutionary struggle, there is a heavy weight to carry. It is demanding a lot of them to play this role, to be the ones to most steadfastly carry the revolutionary struggle along. But it is not too much to demand.

In basketball there are those players who are not only outstanding in general but who specifically make the big plays at the crucial moments. These are the ones who *want* the ball when crunch time comes, when the whole game is on the line. They are the ones who love to go into the home court of the biggest rivals and rise to their greatest right in the face of the other team and their howling, screaming fans. These are the ones who not only soar to great heights themselves but in so doing raise the level of their team as a whole. Why shouldn't the advanced forces of proletarian revolution—those who have the most profound interest in this revolution and the most profound desire for revolution—why shouldn't they be capable of this kind of greatness?

Bullets, From the Writings, Speeches, & Interviews of Bob Avakian, Chairman of the Revolutionary Communist Party, USA, 1985

#4

If you recognize that, as happens, leaders do emerge who play an outstanding role—who represent a concentration of understanding of the way the world

is, and how it can and should be changed, on a higher
level than others around them at a given time—then
that can be a very positive thing. To have something
like that and to recognize it can be a very positive thing.
And it requires people to rally to that and defend it at
the same time as it requires them to come forward and
play their own role in this struggle....

So there's a unity there as well as a contradiction
between, on the one hand, someone who does come
forward who has an advanced understanding and does
concentrate, as I said, on a higher level than others, a
certain understanding of how the world is and how it
could be changed; and on the other hand, the role of a lot
of other people, and growing numbers of people, in taking
up the same approach to changing the world—the same
communist outlook and methodology—and making the
biggest contribution they can to it. And the more that both
those things go on, the further we're going to be ahead.

"On Communism, Leadership, Stalin, and the
Experience of Socialist Society," excerpts transcribed
from a radio interview, *Revolution* #168, June 21, 2009

#5

If you don't have a poetic spirit—or at least a poetic
side—it is very dangerous for you to lead a Marxist
movement or be the leader of a socialist state.

"Materialism and Romanticism: Can We Do Without Myth?"
Observations on Art and Culture, Science and Philosophy, 2005
(quote originally published 1990)

#6

I must confess that, especially in light of the brutal murder of [Peter] Tosh*—the robbing of such a powerful and beautiful voice against injustice—I am filled with an almost overwhelming feeling of sadness and anger every time I listen to this album—and yet, at the same time, a certain sense of triumph in the fact that the music does still go on. In particular, when I listened to Peter Tosh's song "Lessons in My Life"—with its lines about how people make you promises today and tomorrow they change their minds, and how you have to be careful of your friends, because money can make friendship end—I had a very hard time holding back tears....

But what I think is most important to do is to take up the challenge posed: Money can make friendship end. Certainly I do not think that money, as such, will cause us to turn our backs on what we have set out to do and all the people who are—subjectively in some cases already, but objectively in the case of millions and millions of people—counting on us to do what we have set out to do—to lead in doing this. I do not think we will turn back from this, or be turned away from it, because of things like money. But what about egos? What about ways, petty as well as not-so-petty, in which bourgeois relations and ideas permeate every pore of society and encircle us on every side? Will we give in to this? Those sugar-coated bullets are even more destructive than literal bullets, because when someone falls to sugar-coated bullets it is demoralizing to the masses of people beyond the loss of a particular person. Can we resist these sugar-coated bullets, all the way through?...

"I'm a progressive man, and I love progressive people; I'm an honest man, and I love honest people..." This is, profoundly, a just verdict on Tosh. We, of course, have differences with him, in particular that he is (or was) religious and we are against religion, ideologically. But he was one of those of whom it must definitely be said that his religious convictions led him to stand, firmly, with the oppressed of the world against the oppressors. And he did so with sweep and power.

We, with the most far-seeing and thoroughly liberating ideology there is, can learn from this "fired man." We can rise where he rose, and take it still higher. Sadness to anger; anger to intensified revolutionary energy, fired with a profoundly realistic optimism: that is what should drive us forward and lift our spirit and sights.

> From *Ike to Mao and Beyond: My Journey from Mainstream America to Revolutionary Communist, A Memoir* by Bob Avakian; from a letter written by Bob Avakian in the aftermath of Peter Tosh's death, included in his memoir, 2005

* Peter Tosh was a radical, revolutionary-minded reggae singer in the 1970s and '80s who was brutally murdered.

#7

There is a great deal of misunderstanding and confusion about the question of communist leadership, confusion which is bound up to a large degree with misconceptions about—and in some ways opposition to—the principles and objectives of communist revolution itself. Leadership—and in particular communist leadership—is, as I have been speaking to, concentrated in line. This does not simply mean line as theoretical abstractions, although such abstractions, especially insofar as they do correctly reflect reality and its motion and development, are extremely important. But in an all-around sense, it is a matter of leadership as expressed in the ability to continually make essentially correct theoretical abstractions; to formulate, to wield, and to lead others to take up and act on—and to themselves take initiative in wielding—the outlook and method, and the strategy, program, and policies, necessary to radically transform the world through revolution toward the final aim of communism; and through this process to continually enable others one is leading to themselves increasingly develop their ability to do all this. This is the essence of communist leadership.

> *Ruminations and Wranglings: On the Importance of*
> *Marxist Materialism, Communism as a Science,*
> *Meaningful Revolutionary Work, and a Life with Meaning,*
> *Revolution #167, June 7, 2009*

#8

There are these divisions that the historical development of society has brought into being and which capitalism reinforces, not only spontaneously but also by the operation of the ruling class and the institutions of power. These divisions can only be overcome through the advanced forces who have a fundamental understanding of the nature of the problem, and the solution, uniting together as a vanguard force to go out among the masses and bring them forward around this line and programme. Without that, there may be other people who are capable of developing other theories but there will be no revolution, and whatever changes in society are in fact brought about, the masses of people will be left out of it. And you can speak in the name of the masses of people all day long and rail against leadership all day long in the name of the masses, or in the name of some other principle, but if you don't actually recognize the need for leadership, and the fact that it flows out of the very contradictions of the society you're seeking to overturn and transform, then you're going to leave the masses entirely out of the equation and there's not going to be a revolution and certainly not one that leads to the emancipation of the broad masses of people.

Reaching for the Heights and Flying Without a Safety Net,
Revolutionary Worker #1207, July 20, 2003

#9

If you deny the need for vanguard leadership and for leadership even within the party, then you are guaranteeing that bourgeois methods of leadership and bourgeois forms of leadership will prevail. That is the only real choice—proletarian leadership and methods of leadership versus bourgeois—not leadership versus no leadership, not "vanguard vs. no vanguard."

Bullets (quote originally published 1982)

#10

Somebody asked the question: did I think that as a white male I could actually lead the revolution. Well, the answer is no, not as a white male—but I think I could play a leading role in it as a <u>communist</u>.

> "'A New Generation of Revolutionary Leaders':
> Bob Avakian on the Essence of Communist Leadership and
> Bringing Forward New Leaders," *Revolution* #201, May 16, 2010

#11

Why am I—why is my body of work, and method and approach—important? Because this is bringing forward an advanced understanding, a heightened understanding, of what revolution and communism are all about and how to move toward the objective of revolution and communism, as well as a method for engaging and struggling through the contradictions that are inevitably going to be encountered in that process....

If we are in fact being guided by the scientific understanding that human society needs to, and can, advance to communism, that the struggle to achieve this objective must be the conscious act of masses of people, on the one hand, while at the same time this must have, and has no prospect of being realized without, leadership—leadership that, in relation to this goal, embodies the most advanced understanding and methodology—and that

what is concentrated in this person, yes, but most
fundamentally in the body of work and method and
approach of Bob Avakian represents that leadership;
then what flows naturally from that is the recognition
that this is something the masses of people must
be made aware of and acquainted with, and must
take up as their own, with the understanding of
how crucial it is, in terms of their own fundamental
interests and ultimately the highest interests of
humanity as a whole. As a document of our Party on
the question of revolutionary leadership emphasizes:

"the fact that certain individual revolutionaries
emerge as a *concentration* of this process, and
themselves become a concentrated expression of the
best qualities of revolutionary leadership—including
a selfless dedication to the revolutionary cause and
deep love of the masses, as well as a strong grasp
of the scientific methodology needed to unleash the
masses and chart the path of revolution in line with
their objective interests—then the existence of such
an individual leader or leaders is not something to
lament but something to welcome and celebrate! It is
part of the people's strength."

Making Revolution and Emancipating Humanity – Part 2:
"Everything We're Doing Is About Revolution,"
Revolution #115, January 13, 2008

#12

None of the qualities which are required for leadership, or to be a communist in general—none of this is innate. Nor is it genetic. All these qualities are things that are learned, even though they are not, and they cannot be, learned all at once. Developing as a communist, like everything else, is a process and it proceeds through waves or spirals. And it is marked by being repeatedly confronted with the need to make leaps and ruptures at critical junctures when the challenges become particularly acute. Different people have different particular experiences—both personal experiences and the larger social experiences in which these personal experiences occur—and this leads to different people having different strengths and weaknesses. What our orientation should be, both in terms of leadership and in terms of the broader Party and the broader masses, is one of combining all positive factors, as Mao put it—helping people to build on their strengths and overcome their weaknesses, even while recognizing that not all people are going to have the same strengths or the same weaknesses. Nor would it be possible or desirable to live in a world where everybody had exactly the same strengths and the same weaknesses. That would, in fact, be impossible—and it would be an awful world if it were possible.

Reaching for the Heights and Flying Without a Safety Net,
Revolutionary Worker #1205, June 29, 2003

#13

Editor's note: The following are comments made by Bob Avakian in 2008 about the Cultural Revolution within the Revolutionary Communist Party, USA—a major ideological struggle he initiated and led in which the question was sharply posed: whether the Party would continue to advance on the revolutionary road or, instead, adopt a stance that essentially gave up on revolution and settled for a place within the existing system.

As I saw and confronted things at the time, more or less 5 years ago, there were three basic choices when it became clear that, despite the continuing revolutionary-communist character of the Party's "official" line, the Party was in fact "saturated with" and even characterized by revisionism. The three choices were:

accept this Party as it was, and in essence give up on what the Party is *supposed* to be all about;

quit, and set out to start a new Party;

or, launch the Cultural Revolution.

I believed then, and still believe now, for reasons I've spoken to elsewhere and earlier today, that the *latter* course was the only correct course and the necessary course. This is for reasons having to do with how precious a party is, and how difficult it would be to create a new party if in fact prematurely and incorrectly this Party were given up on. But, yes, it is true, there is nothing holy about a party, and if it's not going to be a revolutionary vanguard, then

fuck it!—let's do something else and get something
else. But I believed then, and I believe now, that we
must not give up on this Party unless objectively and
scientifically it is clearly indicated that there is no
hope for actually transforming this Party into what it
needs to be.

As quoted in *Communism: The Beginning of a New Stage,
A Manifesto from the Revolutionary Communist Party, USA*, 2008

#14

The essential challenge that we face, not just in a
general and historical sense, but very urgently—the
question that is posed, not only in an overall strategic
sense but also immediately and acutely—is one of being
the vanguard of the future, or at best the residue of
the past. And the dimensions and the stakes of this are
constantly increasing.

This applies to our Party. It involves the question
of being, in a sense, real, concentrated expressions
of the emancipators of humanity and leaders of
emancipators of humanity. And the same challenge
applies on the international level to the communist
movement and in terms of the internationalist
responsibilities of communists.

Are we going to go down as a residue of the past and
another disappointment and in fact another arrow
in the back of the masses of people? Or, without
any guarantees of victory in any particular set of

circumstances but with strategic objectives and a
sweeping view in mind, are we going to rise to the
challenge of being, together with our comrades
throughout the world, the vanguard of the future?

Bringing Forward Another Way, *Revolution* #100, September 9, 2007

#15

What we are setting out to do, and the principles
and methods involved in this, are not a matter
of *apriorism* and instrumentalism—we know the
answers to everything going in, and it's simply a
matter of reconfiguring things so that everybody
we're working with gives us the right answers when
we pose the right questions. To the degree that there
are tendencies in this direction, it is something we
have to thoroughly rupture with and root out. We
must be engaging reality, on as scientific a basis
as we possibly can, at any given time. And, in this
process, we are interacting with other people who are
applying different outlooks and different approaches
with different objectives. Their thinking, their
objectives, their inclinations and their ideas—some
of which may actually better reflect reality than our
understanding at times and with regard to certain
phenomena, lest we forget—this is also part of the
larger objective reality that we need to engage. It
is necessary to have a scientific approach to that as
well. We need to have a systematically, consistently,
and comprehensively scientific approach to

everything—and the communist outlook and method provides the means to do that, *if* we actually take up and apply it, and don't corrupt it with religious or other philosophically idealist and metaphysical notions and approaches.

This is why I like the image, or metaphor, of our being a team of scientists—scientists setting out to transform the world in the most profound way. What we're about is not anything different than that. So we have to be consistently and thoroughly scientific ourselves, even when we're interacting with many people who are anything but that—or are that at certain times and to a certain degree, but then again are not scientific in the most consistent, systematic, and comprehensive sense.

Making Revolution and Emancipating Humanity – Part 1:
"Beyond the Narrow Horizon of Bourgeois Right,"
Revolution #109, November 18, 2007

#16

Would the best of Bob Dylan have been brought forward, if we had led that step by step, especially if we had done this in a narrow, reformist, and kind of "workerist" way, and an instrumentalist way, insisting that every artistic creation have some direct and "linear" relation to politics and in particular the immediate political struggles of the day? NO! So then, does that mean we don't need model works that are really models? No. We do need those things. And there are artists who will be willing to work with

us in that way, especially if we work correctly with
them. But that is not *all* we need. Life is much more
rich—that is the point Lenin was making when he
emphasized that the tree of life is much more green
than that. Communism does spring from every pore,
as Lenin also emphasized; but this won't happen if
we "stop up" every pore with a pitiful dogmatist
caricature of communism and communist leadership
and methods. Even what's not communism can
contribute to communism *if* we know how to lead
correctly. If we know how to correctly apply "solid
core with a lot of elasticity."

> "Art and Artistic Creation – Solid Core with a Lot of Elasticity,"
> *Observations on Art and Culture, Science and Philosophy,* 2005

#17

There is always change, of one kind or another, and
there has been and will again be <u>major</u> change in the
world and in human society. Society, like all material
reality, cannot and does not stay as it is. It goes
through changes, including at certain points major,
even qualitative, changes. But the question of line and
leadership is decisive in determining ultimately what
<u>kind</u> of change, what <u>kind</u> of transformation of society
and fundamentally what <u>kind</u> of revolution is going to
be possible, even if and when the masses do rise up and
demand and fight for radical change.

> *Ruminations and Wranglings, Revolution* #167, June 7, 2009

#18

When I look at all this, I think again of my friend who
decided to dedicate his life to ending cancer—and
of the even greater need to put an end to the system
of capitalism-imperialism and all the suffering and
oppression this system embodies and enforces
throughout the world. You see that there isn't anything
more important that your life could be about, and
whatever you end up contributing during the course
of your lifetime is the most important and the most
uplifting thing that you could possibly do. And yes,
there are moments of great disappointment, but also
moments of great joy as part of this. There is the joy that
comes from seeing the ways in which people break free
of constraints and rise up and begin to see the world as
it really is and take up more consciously the struggle to
change it. There is the joy of knowing that you are part
of this whole process and contributing what you can to
it. There is the joy of the camaraderie of being together
with others in this struggle and knowing that it is
something worthwhile, that it is not something petty and
narrow that you are involved in but something uplifting.
There is the joy of looking to the future and envisioning
the goal that you are struggling for and seeing people
come to even a beginning understanding of what that
could mean, not just for themselves but for society, for
humanity as a whole.

So this is what my life will continue to be devoted to, and this is what the ongoing story of my life will be about.

From Ike to Mao and Beyond

#19

In conclusion I want to put forward a challenge and a call. Get with this. Get with the Party. If you're already with this, get with it even deeper. Take it up even more fully and firmly in an even more conscious and determined way....Let people know who do not know yet that they have a vanguard party, and what this means for the masses of people here and all over the world. Let them know that with this vanguard party, there is a way out of all this madness and needless suffering and misery. As for people who are learning of this, the challenge is to get tighter with the Party, and then to come into the Party and help strengthen and build it as a revolutionary vanguard the proletariat and masses of people so deeply need. Take our revolutionary line and vision, our understanding of the world and our method for understanding the world, and our program and plan for changing the world through revolution. Take this to ever growing numbers of people and struggle to win them to this. Build resistance and organization among all sections of the people and work to link this more and more closely with the Party. Take the line of the Party everywhere,

everywhere people are fighting back, everywhere they are questioning: Does the world have to be like this? Everywhere they are suffering but are searching or even hoping for a way out. Everywhere they talk about how we need some kind of real change. And especially where they say that we need some kind of revolution. Move them to see how revolution is possible, what this revolution is all about and how it can and must be prepared for and carried out....We should in a real way be on a mission with this and everyone should seek to contribute in whatever way they can to this.

Revolution: Why It's Necessary, Why It's Possible, What It's All About, a film of a talk by Bob Avakian. Available at revolutiontalk.net and in a DVD set from RCP Publications.

Supplement

The Revolutionary Potential of the Masses and the Responsibility of the Vanguard

Editor's note: The following article by Bob Avakian appeared in *Revolutionary Worker* #1270, March 13, 2005.

One of the things that I see, something that I haven't lost sight of, is this: I see all the strength of the ruling class, but I also see all the way through all this shit, all the contradictions in society—I actually see a force in this society that, if it were developed into a revolutionary people, actually could have a go at it, could have a real chance of making a revolution, or being the backbone force of a revolution, when the conditions were ripe. I see a force of millions and millions and millions—youth and others—for whom this system is a horror: It isn't going to take some cataclysmic crisis for this system to be fucking over them. The ruling class, ironically, sees them too. It is those who once had but have lost—or those who never had—a revolutionary perspective...it is they who can't see this.

So what I'm working on is all the things that are in between that revolutionary potential and its actual realization. How does this force of masses at the base of society get joined by people from other strata, how does it get allies broadly, how does it get "friendly neutrality" among many in the middle strata—how does all this get developed into a revolutionary people that can become a powerful fighting force when the conditions emerge to fight all out for the seizure of power? How does all that happen *not in a passive sense*, but *how do we work on* bringing this revolutionary people into being, even if most of the changes in society and the world are not owing to our initiative but to larger objective factors? I actually believe there is such a revolutionary force in potential—I actually believe this, I see this potential—I believe that there is a force there that, if somehow (and the bourgeoisie knows this too) if somehow the bourgeoisie got into a real, deep crisis....

Yes, these masses have got a lot of ideological hang-ups, and everything else—that's why we have work to do— but we should never lose sight of that potential. And it's not only the oppressed nationalities either—although that is a good part of it, it's not the whole of it. There are a lot of youth, and there are a lot of other masses, of all nationalities. They are not a revolutionary people now, and they are not joined by other forces in the way they need to be—they don't have the necessary allies, they don't have the necessary "friendly neutrality," they don't have the political paralysis of the half-hearted reformist trends, and whatever. But that relates to the crucial question of *where we come in*, in relation to all that. Do we just wait for "the stars to all align"? Or do we have a lot we can do—is there a lot of back and forth between us and the objective situation, not just at the point of a revolutionary crisis but all along the way toward that point?

This is why, among other things, I haven't become discouraged with all these twists and turns. Not only do I have the moral dimension of feeling it's an outrage the way that masses of people, tens of millions in the U.S. and literally billions more in the world, are treated, but I'm also thinking about how to bring into being this revolutionary people—not just how are they going to become a revolutionary people in the sense of wanting to make revolution and overthrowing the system, but how are they going to become a revolutionary people in terms of "fitting themselves to rule" as Marx once put it. This is why I don't feel like tailing them—because what good is that doing for them?

I told some people in a discussion recently: If anybody expects that, because I'm a white male, I am going to be apologetic about putting myself forward as a leader, they are going to be terribly disappointed—you are in for a big disappointment if you expect me to be apologetic about that. Because whom are we thinking about when we're thinking that way? And *what* are we thinking about? Are we really thinking about the masses of people who are bitterly oppressed, and what they need to get out from that oppression, and to make a whole different, much better world—or are we thinking about something else? That's why I don't feel like tailing these masses. There are plenty of people pandering to them and using them in various ways, and feeling sorry for them. I *hate* the way the masses of people suffer, but I don't feel sorry for them. They have the potential to remake the world, and we have to struggle like hell with them to get them to see that and to get them to rise to that. We shouldn't aim for anything less. Why should we think they are capable of anything less?

And, yes, there are a tremendous number of contradictions. I'm not an idealist—I'm not a "soft-headed liberal"—I know that the masses of people have real limitations and shortcomings, as a result of living and struggling to survive under this system. Many of them have been denied not only formal education but access to knowledge about many spheres—and a good number of them have even been denied the means to learn basic things, like how to read—but that doesn't mean they are not capable of overcoming all this. And it doesn't mean that they have not accumulated a great deal of experience and knowledge and wisdom of many kinds, which can contribute to the development of the revolutionary struggle, especially as this is taken up by people wielding a scientific communist outlook and method and spreading *this* among the masses of people. We should understand, on a scientific basis, that these masses are fully capable of becoming conscious communist revolutionaries. Those who have been kept illiterate by this system are capable of being leaders of a revolution and of a new society that will overcome the things that made them illiterate. We should struggle like hell, ideologically and practically, to enable them to become literate; but, even if they don't, they can still play a leading role in the revolution. You want to talk about the non-professional leading the professional? This is how you do it—you do it with ideology, communist ideology and methodology, in the fullest sense. And you do it with *the correct understanding* of this ideology. Some of the masses who are going to play leading roles in this process are never going to understand much beyond some basic things about physics, for example. And most of us here aren't either. But they don't have to understand all that to be able to lead. If you have the right ideology and methodology, you can still relate correctly to physics, and to physicists, and to people in all these spheres. You can still enable the masses to enter into these spheres and learn about them, and learn how to give leadership, in an overall sense politically and ideologically, to people in these spheres—without undermining and undercutting these spheres, without acting in a narrow way, or worse yet a tyrannical way, towards the people who *do* have specialized knowledge and expertise in these spheres, and without limiting and constricting them but, on the contrary, valuing and learning from them and their knowledge—*and their search for knowledge*—and uniting and struggling in a good way with them. It's tough, we have to work on these problems some more, but there is a methodology here that can lead to correctly dealing with these contradictions, in a way that gives full expression to the scientific method, the scientific spirit and scientific inquiry, to the flowering of the imagination and the search for the truth, and that leads all this to serve the emancipation and the betterment of humanity.

And, at the same time, it is very important to keep in mind that more than a few physicists, and people with expertise in other fields, will themselves become communists and play leading roles, not only in relation to their particular area of expertise but in an overall sense, in making revolution and transforming all of society and bringing a whole new world into being.

Masses of different strata, including the basic masses—we cannot have the idea that they are capable of less than they are capable of. They are capable of terrible things, yes; some do terrible things, too, as a result of what this system has done to them; but that doesn't mean that this is somehow their "essence" and all that they are capable of. Speaking of the broad masses, including some who have gotten caught up in terrible things, they are also capable of *great* things.

It is the responsibility of those who are the vanguard to lead the masses to realize this potential, to become a revolutionary people and, when the time becomes ripe, to be the backbone of a revolution that will open up the way to a whole better world. And, yes, that means struggling with the masses to, first of all, recognize their own revolutionary potential, their potential to become the emancipators of humanity, and then to act in accordance with that potential.

SELECTED BIBLIOGRAPHY
Updated April 2013

For the complete talks and writings from which this book is drawn, go to:

Film and Audio by Bob Avakian

Film

BA Speaks: REVOLUTION—NOTHING LESS! Bob Avakian Live. Film of a talk given in 2012. For more on this film and to order the DVD set, go to revcom.us.

Revolution: Why It's Necessary, Why It's Possible, What It's All About, a film of a talk by Bob Avakian (2003). Available through revcom.us.

Audio

Bob Avakian, interviewed by Cornel West on the *Smiley & West* show, Public Radio International, October 2012. Available at revcom.us.

Bob Avakian, five part interview on *The Michael Slate Show*, KPFK Radio, Los Angeles, January and February 2013. Available at revcom.us.

7 Talks (2006)
1. Why We're in the Situation We're in Today...And What to Do About It: A Thoroughly Rotten System and the Need for Revolution
2. Communism and Jeffersonian Democracy
3. Communism: A Whole New World and the Emancipation of All Humanity—Not "The Last Shall Be First, and The First Shall Be Last"
4. The NBA: Marketing the Minstrel Show and Serving the Big Gangsters
5. Communism and Religion: Getting Up and Getting Free— Making Revolution to Change the Real World, Not Relying on "Things Unseen"
6. Conservatism, Christian Fundamentalism, Liberalism and Paternalism...Bill Cosby and Bill Clinton... Not All "Right" But All Wrong!
7. "Balance" Is the Wrong Criterion—and a Cover for a Witch-hunt—What We Need Is the Search for the Truth: Education, Real Academic Freedom, Critical Thinking and Dissent

Question and Answer Session, with Concluding Remarks
Available at revcom.us.

"All Played Out" (spoken word piece with words by Bob Avakian and music by William Parker), Centeringmusic BMI, 2011. Available at revcom.us and soundcloud.com/allplayedout.

Books, Articles, and Other Written Works by Bob Avakian

Advancing the World Revolutionary Movement: Questions of Strategic Orientation, Revolution magazine, RCP Publications, Spring 1984. Available at revcom.us.

"Art and Artistic Creation—Solid Core with a Lot of Elasticity," *Observations on Art and Culture, Science and Philosophy* (Insight Press, 2005).

Away With All Gods! Unchaining the Mind and Radically Changing the World (Insight Press, 2008).

"The Basis, the Goals, and the Methods of the Communist Revolution." From a talk given in 2005. *Revolution*, May 2006–January 2007. Available at revcom.us.

Birds Cannot Give Birth to Crocodiles, But Humanity Can Soar Beyond the Horizon. From a talk given in 2010.
    Part 1: "Revolution and the State," *Revolution*, 2010-2011.
    Part 2: "Building the Movement for Revolution," *Revolution*, 2011. Available at revcom.us.

"Bob Avakian in a Discussion with Comrades on Epistemology: On Knowing and Changing the World," *Revolutionary Worker* #1262, December 19, 2004. Available at revcom.us. Also in *Observations on Art and Culture, Science and Philosophy* (Insight Press, 2005).

Bringing Forward Another Way. From a talk given in 2006. *Revolution*, March–September 2007. Available at revcom.us and as a pamphlet from RCP Publications.

Bullets, From the Writings, Speeches, & Interviews of Bob Avakian, Chairman of the Revolutionary Communist Party, USA (RCP Publications, 1985).

"The 'City Game'—And the City, No Game," *Revolutionary Worker* #201, April 15, 1983. Also in *Reflections, Sketches & Provocations: Essays and Commentary, 1981-1987* (RCP Publications, 1990).

The Coming Civil War and Repolarization for Revolution in the Present Era, Revolution, March–September 2005. Also available as a pamphlet (RCP Publications, 2005) and at revcom.us.

Communism and Jeffersonian Democracy (RCP Publications, 2008). Available at revcom.us.

Communists Are Rebels: A Letter from RCP Chairman Bob Avakian to His Parents on Philosophy, Religion, Morals, and Continuous Revolution (Revolutionary Communist Youth, April 1980).

Conquer the World? The International Proletariat Must and Will, *Revolution* magazine, RCP Publications, December 1981. Available at revcom.us.

"'Crises in Physics,' Crises in Philosophy and Politics," *Revolution* #161, April 12, 2009. Available at revcom.us. Also in *Demarcations: A Journal of Communist Theory and Polemic*, Issue Number 1, Summer-Fall 2009. Available at demarcations-journal.org.

"The Deadly Illusion of the Swinging Pendulum," *Revolution* #20, October 20, 2005. Available at revcom.us.

Democracy: Can't We Do Better Than That? (Banner Press, 1986).

Dictatorship and Democracy, and the Socialist Transition to Communism. From a talk given in 2004. *Revolutionary Worker*, August 2004–January 2005. Available at revcom.us.

"The End of a Stage—The Beginning of a New Stage," *Revolution* magazine, RCP Publications, Fall 1990.

"A Final Note: Principles in Carrying Forward the Revolution Under the Dictatorship of the Proletariat and Preventing Revisionism and the Rise to Power of the (New) Bourgeoisie," *Revolution* magazine, RCP Publications, Fall 1990.

For a Harvest of Dragons: On the "Crisis of Marxism" and the Power of Marxism—Now More Than Ever (RCP Publications, 1983).

From Ike to Mao and Beyond: My Journey from Mainstream America to Revolutionary Communist, A Memoir by Bob Avakian (Insight Press, 2005). Excerpts in *Revolution*, available at revcom.us. Audio of Bob Avakian reading selections from this memoir are at revcom.us.

Getting Over the Two Great Humps: Further Thoughts on Conquering the World. Excerpts in *Revolutionary Worker*, October 1997–January 1998 (under the series title "Getting Over the Hump") and October 2003–January 2004 (under the title "On Proletarian Democracy and Proletarian Dictatorship—A Radically Different View of Leading Society"). Available at revcom.us.

Grasp Revolution, Promote Production: Questions of Outlook and Method, Some Points on the New Situation. From a talk given in 2002. Excerpts in *Revolutionary Worker*, November 2002–March 2003. Available at revcom.us.

A Horrible End, or An End to the Horror? (RCP Publications, 1984).

"In the Wake of the Election, a Basic Point of Orientation: To the Masses...With Revolution," *Revolution* #149, November 30, 2008.

"'A Leap of Faith' and a Leap to Rational Knowledge: Two Very Different Kinds of Leaps, Two Radically Different Worldviews and Methods," *Revolution* #10, July 31, 2005. Available at revcom.us.

Making Revolution and Emancipating Humanity
    Part 1: "Beyond the Narrow Horizon of Bourgeois Right"
    Part 2: "Everything We're Doing Is About Revolution"
Revolution, October 2007–February 2008. Available at revcom.us, and also included in *Revolution and Communism: A Foundation and Strategic Orientation,* a *Revolution* pamphlet, 2008.

Marxism and the Call of the Future: Conversations on Ethics, History, and Politics (with Bill Martin, Open Court Publishing, 2005).

"Materialism and Romanticism: Can We Do Without Myth?" *Observations on Art and Culture, Science and Philosophy* (Insight Press, 2005).

"Methods and Principles," *Observations on Art and Culture, Science and Philosophy* (Insight Press, 2005).

"'A New Generation of Revolutionary Leaders': Bob Avakian on the Essence of Communist Leadership, and Bringing Forward New Leaders," *Revolution* #201, May 16, 2010, transcribed from the talk *Revolution: Why It's Necessary, Why It's Possible, What It's All About.* Available at revcom.us.

Observations on Art and Culture, Science and Philosophy (Insight Press, 2005).

"On Communism, Leadership, Stalin, and the Experience of Socialist Society," excerpts transcribed from a radio interview, *Revolution* #168, June 21, 2009. Available at revcom.us.

"The Oppression of Black People & The Revolutionary Struggle To End All Oppression," a series of excerpts from writings and talks by Bob Avakian published in *Revolution* during Black History Month, February 2007. Available at revcom.us.

Out Into the World—As a Vanguard of the Future. From a talk given in 2008. *Revolution,* February–April 2009. Available at revcom.us.

Phony Communism Is Dead...Long Live Real Communism! (RCP Publications, 1992; Second Edition with Appendix *Democracy: More Than Ever We Can and Must Do Better Than That,* 2004).

Preaching From a Pulpit of Bones, We Need Morality, But Not Traditional *Morality* (Banner Press, 1999).

"Putting Forward Our Line in a Bold, Moving, Compelling Way," published in two parts in *Revolutionary Worker*: Part 1, #1177, December 1, 2002; Part 2, #1178, December 8, 2002. Available at revcom.us.

Reaching for the Heights and Flying Without a Safety Net. From a talk given in 2002. *Revolutionary Worker*, April–August 2003. Available at revcom.us.

Reflections, Sketches & Provocations: Essays and Commentary, 1981-1987 (RCP Publications, 1990).

"Reform or Revolution: Questions of Orientation, Questions of Morality," *Revolution* #32, January 29, 2006. Available at revcom.us.

"The Revolutionary Potential of the Masses and the Responsibility of the Vanguard," *Revolutionary Worker* #1270, March 13, 2005. Available at revcom.us.

"The Role of Dissent in a Vibrant Society," *Observations on Art and Culture, Science and Philosophy* (Insight Press, 2005).

Ruminations and Wranglings: On the Importance of Marxist Materialism, Communism as a Science, Meaningful Revolutionary Work, and a Life with Meaning. From a talk given in 2009. *Revolution*, May–September 2009. Available at revcom.us.

"Slavery: Yesterday and Today," *Revolution* #78, February 11, 2007. Available at revcom.us.

"Some Observations on the Culture Wars: Textbooks, Movies, Sham Shakespearean Tragedies and Crude Lies," *Revolution* #198, April 11, 2010. Available at revcom.us.

"Some Principles for Building a Movement for Revolution," *Revolution* #202, May 17, 2010. Available at revcom.us.

"Statement by Bob Avakian, Chairman of the Revolutionary Communist Party, on the Occasion of the Death of Willie 'Mobile' Shaw," *Revolution* #27, December 18, 2005. Available at revcom.us.

Strategic Questions, excerpts published in *Revolutionary Worker*, 1996-1997 and 2002. Available at revcom.us.

"There Is No 'Permanent Necessity' for Things To Be This Way: A Radically Different and Better World Can Be Brought Into Being Through Revolution," *Revolution* #198, April 11, 2010. Available at revcom.us.

"Three Alternative Worlds," *Revolution* #77, January 28, 2007. Available at revcom.us. Also in *Observations on Art and Culture, Science and Philosophy* (Insight Press, 2005).

Unresolved Contradictions, Driving Forces for Revolution
Part I: "Once More on the Coming Civil War... and Repolarization for Revolution"
Part II: "(Some Observations on) The International Movement"
Part III: "The New Synthesis and the Woman Question: The Emancipation of Women and the Communist Revolution—Further Leaps and Radical Ruptures"
Revolution, November 2009–April 2010. Entire talk available at revcom.us.

"Views on Socialism and Communism: A Radically New Kind of State, A Radically Different and Far Greater Vision of Freedom." From a talk given in 2005. *Revolution*, March–April 2006. Available at revcom.us.

"We Can't Know Everything—So We Should Be Good at Learning," *Revolutionary Worker* #1181, December 29, 2002 (part of a series of excerpts from the talk *Grasp Revolution, Promote Production: Questions of Outlook and Method, Some Points on the New Situation*). Available at revcom.us. Also in *Observations on Art and Culture, Science and Philosophy* (Insight Press, 2005).

What Humanity Needs: Revolution, and the New Synthesis of Communism, An Interview with Bob Avakian by A. Brooks. May 1, 2012. Available at revcom.us and as a pamphlet from RCP Publications.

Other Key Works Published by the Revolutionary Communist Party, USA

Communism: The Beginning of a New Stage, A Manifesto from the Revolutionary Communist Party, USA, September 2008 (RCP Publications, 2009). Available at revcom.us.

Constitution for the New Socialist Republic in North America (Draft Proposal) (RCP Publications, 2010). Available at revcom.us.

Constitution of the Revolutionary Communist Party, USA (RCP Publications, 2008). Available at revcom.us.

1995 Leadership Resolutions on Leaders and Leadership:
Part I: The Party Exists for No Other Reason than to Serve the Masses, to Make Revolution
Part II: Some Points on the Question of Revolutionary Leadership and Individual Leaders
Revolutionary Worker #825, October 1, 1995. Available at revcom.us.

"On the Strategy for Revolution," *Revolution* #226, March 6, 2011. Available at revcom.us.

Revolution, national weekly English/Spanish bilingual newspaper of the Revolutionary Communist Party, USA (previously published as *Revolutionary Worker* from 1979-2005). RCP Publications. Available at revcom.us.

Revolution and Communism: A Foundation and Strategic Orientation. A *Revolution* pamphlet (reprints from *Revolution* newspaper), May 1, 2008. Includes:
    Making Revolution and Emancipating Humanity, by Bob Avakian
        Part 1: "Beyond the Narrow Horizon of Bourgeois Right"
        Part 2: "Everything We're Doing Is About Revolution"
    "On the Possibility of Revolution," Letter from a Reader and Response, originally published *Revolution* #102, September 23, 2007
    Appendix: "Some Crucial Points of Revolutionary Orientation in Opposition to Infantile Posturing and Distortions of Revolution"

Some Other Important Works Referred to in this Book

Demarcations: A Journal of Communist Theory and Polemic, Issue Number 1, Summer-Fall 2009. demarcations-journal.org.

Frederick Engels, *Anti-Dühring*, 1878 (Peking: Foreign Languages Press, 1976).

V. I. Lenin, *What Is To Be Done?*, 1902 (Peking: Foreign Languages Press, 1973).

Mao Tsetung, "On Practice," 1937, in *Selected Works*, Volume 1 (Peking: Foreign Languages Press, 1975).

Karl Marx, *The Class Struggles in France, 1848-50*, in *Marx-Engels Selected Works*, Volume 1, 1895.

Karl Marx and Frederick Engels, *Manifesto of the Communist Party*, 1848 (Peking: Foreign Languages Press, 1977).

RCP Writing Group, *On the Position on Homosexuality in the New Draft Programme*, prepared in 2001 by a specially constituted writing group assembled by the RCP, USA. Available at revcom.us.

Ardea Skybreak, *The Science of Evolution and the Myth of Creationism —Knowing What's Real and Why It Matters* (Insight Press, 2006).

ABOUT THE AUTHOR

Bob Avakian is the Chairman of the Revolutionary Communist Party, USA. For more on Bob Avakian and his works, go to revcom.us.